QUIZZING: EVERYTHING YOU ALWAYS WANTED TO KNOW, BUT DIDN'T KNOW WHERE TO LOOK

THE ULTIMATE TRIVIA BOOK

Ranjit Thomas

Writers Club Press
San Jose New York Lincoln Shanghai

**Quizzing: Everything You Always Wanted to Know,
But Didn't Know Where to Look**
The Ultimate Trivia Book

Published by Writers Club Press
an imprint of iUniverse.com, Inc.

For information address:
iUniverse.com, Inc.
620 North 48th Street
Suite 201
Lincoln, NE 68504-3467
www.iuniverse.com

ISBN: 0-595-00571-3

Printed in the United States of America

To James Daly

Contents

What is Quizzing?

As a hobby that cuts across all barriers of age, region and sex, nothing compares to quizzing. It definitely isn't the king of hobbies or the hobby of kings–they probably wouldn't be very good at it anyway, given their cramped lifestyles! But in terms of sheer excitement and gratification, it would be difficult to find anything to match it. Above all, if you become a good quizzer, your knowledge about this world will become so vast and intensive, that you will be able to hold your own in any conversation or interview.

What is a quiz anyway? In its simplest form, it is an event in which a quizmaster asks a set of questions, which participants attempt to answer. The queries can be on any topic under the sun, and that is what makes it so challenging. Depending on the format, it could be individuals competing against each other (as in the TV show *Jeopardy*), or teams pitted against one another. In buzzer rounds, the team or individual that first presses the buzzer gets a crack at the answer, so instinct and fast recall play an important part in doing well. Another format that has been popularized by *Who Wants to Be a Millionaire*, involves an individual participant attempting to answer questions that become increasingly more difficult.

Contrary to popular perception, a good memory is not a precondition for this pastime. Quizzing is not about the bland recollection of facts, which unfortunately, it has been reduced to in many quizzes. Rather, quizzing is about building an extensive knowledge base, and using that to work out the answer to questions. The questions themselves, should ideally be ones that have a certain charm about them–interesting and thought provoking.

How Does One Become a Good Quizzer?

The first step towards becoming a good quizzer, is to be knowledgeable, and anything that can contribute to this end would be useful. Reading–newspapers, magazines, books, etc.–would be the single most important thing that one can do. Listening to music, watching television and traveling will also help. Keeping one's eyes and ears open all the time is the key. In addition, attending and participating in quizzes provide valuable experience.

Listening to, or reading a question carefully, and connecting it to your knowledge is important. It is unlikely that you would have come across a question in exactly the same form in which it is presented. Attempting to figure out things and making intelligent guesses will take you a long way. Even the most innocuous words can sometimes give valuable clues. Take the following question, for example, which has been split up into its component parts for the purpose of illustration.

1.   This sport developed in Scotland about a thousand years ago from a Roman game called *Paganica*, which was played with a bent stick and a rubber ball stuffed with feathers.

2.   King James II banned it in 1457 because its popularity threatened the practice of archery, which was needed for the defense of the nation.

3.   It, however, survived and was even played on the moon in February 1971 by Alan Shepard, the commander of the Apollo XIV spacecraft.

4.   Which evergreen sport is this?

From the first clue, it is clear that the game is probably still played with a stick and a ball. Could it be hockey, or croquet, perhaps? It isn't quite clear. The second clue tells us that it wasn't a particularly useful pastime! The third sentence, on close inspection is revealing. If an astronaut could play it on the moon, it obviously isn't a team game, and neither is it a sport that is played between two people, like tennis or squash. If you still haven't been able to work out what it is, go on to the last clue. Why has the word "evergreen" been inserted there? Is it because the sport has always been popular, or is there something more to it? Perhaps, "green" has something to do with the answer. Why, the sport has to be golf, of course! A quick check shows that it is in agreement with the other clues. Remember, if you had known that golf had evolved from Paganica, that it had been banned by some monarch in medieval times, or that it had been played on the moon, that alone would have been sufficient to get you to the answer. Nevertheless, even without that knowledge, just logical thinking could have sufficed.

Many quiz shows require participation in teams of 2-4 members. Here, more than individual brilliance, it is the constituents of the team complementing each other that is the key to doing well. Overlap between members can spell disaster for a team whose individual members may be very good.

What is a "Good" Question?

A good quiz question is one that you'd rack your brains to try and figure out the answer to, and finally when you hear it, say, "Hey, that's interesting!" Or it could be something that's contrary to what you had expected, prompting a "I didn't know that!" A good question does not test your memory, rather it tests your knowledge. The answer should preferably be something or someone well known. Everything obscure should be contained within the question itself, to act as a clue. Obviously, this means that asking for dates and the like is a strict no.

Trivial Pursuit

There's nothing like trivia to satiate one's appetite for fascinating facts. If you're one of this kind, then delve into the following questions.

1. One night in about 1780, James Daly, a manager of a theater in Dublin, laid a wager that he would introduce into the language within twenty-four hours, a new word with a new meaning. Accordingly, on every accessible wall, he chalked up four mystic letters, and the next morning all Dublin was inquiring what they meant. What were those four letters that he inscribed on the walls of the city?

2. Spinach is supposed to contain a lot of iron—a reason given by many mothers to make their kids gulp down that last spoonful. However, it actually has only a tenth of the iron it was originally thought to have. How did this misconception arise?

3. One of the signers of the Declaration of Independence in 1776, Francis Hopkinson, was a notorious doodler. One day, while toying with the year 1776, he came up with an idea, which he submitted to the United States Congress, which liked and approved it. What was his concept, which has been used ever since?

4. The longest word that can be formed using only the top row of a typewriter is "rupturewort," the name of a plant. What is the second longest word that can be thus formed?

5. What is a bobblogesture? Clue: If you're a student, you should know!

6. What does Dr. Thomas Harvey, a former Princeton pathologist, have in a jar of formaldehyde?

7. What peculiarity is referred to as "Caesar's last breath"?

8. You must be quite familiar with Archimedes' Law–the one whose discovery prompted the person concerned to jump out of his bathtub and run naked through the streets. However, do you know what its modern day version, the New Archimedes' Law, is?

9. This pattern was invented in 1873 and modeled on the wings of the American Golden Eagle, symbolizing freedom. Which pattern is this, which many people like to have behind them?

10. The shortest correspondence on record is that between Victor Hugo and his publisher Hurst and Blackett in 1862. Hugo was on holiday and wanted to know how his new novel *Les Miserables* was selling. He wrote "?" What was his publisher's reply?

11. Shortly after x-rays were discovered, some hucksters (economic opportunists operating on the streets) brought out a product, which made them a quick fortune. What was it?

12. Why do people say "Cheers" before drinking?

13. The film *Silent Movie* directed by Mel Brooks has the shortest dialogue script ever. The only spoken word in the film is the French word "*Non.*" Who was it uttered by?

14. Whenever we think of Santa Claus, we imagine him to be a jolly, rotund, red-suited, white whiskered person. However, in earlier times, Santa Claus was pictured by artists in red or green, or dressed in animal furs, and sometimes even with horns. The modern look of Santa Claus was conceived by a Swedish commercial artist named Harry Sundblom, working in Chicago,

who created an advertisement with Santa Claus, to promote a certain product. What was this product?

Answers

1.   QUIZ. The story is apocryphal, but it makes a good beginning for a quiz book!

2.   When the scientists who first conducted the studies to find out the amount of iron in spinach published their findings, they put the decimal point in the wrong place!

3.   Hopkinson added the figures 1,7,7, and 6 and found that they totaled twenty-one. He thus got the idea for a twenty-one gun salute for Presidents, which is now used all over the world.

4.   Typewriter, itself!

5.   The classroom activity of not knowing the answer to the question posed by the teacher, but still raising one's hand so as not to appear dumb. This is done after determining that a sufficient number of others have also raised their hands, so the likelihood of one being asked to give the answer is low.

6.   Albert Einstein's brain!

7.   By a unique coincidence, the number of molecules of air in one lungful is equal to the number of lung equivalents of air in the world. From the time of Caesar's last gasp, all the molecules exhaled would have been dispersed uniformly. Hence, every breath you take is likely to contain one molecule from Caesar's last breath!

8.   If a body is partially or fully immersed in water, the telephone rings!

9.   The arcuate, the design on the back pocket of Levi's jeans.

10.   "!"

11.   X-ray proof underwear. Soon after the sensational discovery of the penetrating power of the rays, many people were afraid of their modesty being outraged by unscrupulous adventurers!

12.   We have five sense organs—skin, nose, tongue, eyes and ears. While drinking, the lips touch the drink, the nose smells it, the tongue tastes it and the eyes see it. The ear doesn't play any part, so to involve this fifth sense, the practice of saying "Cheers" before drinking originated.

13.   Marcel Marceau, the great mime artiste!

14.   Coca-Cola. Sundblom chose red with white trimmings, because those were the Coca-Cola colors. Santa Claus was portrayed as jolly and good-natured because it was a device to encourage people to drink Coke all year round.

Art for Art's Sake

From the earliest times, painting has been one of man's greatest arts. It has come a long way since he first drew figures and events on the walls of caves. Today, paintings sell for millions and are bought not just to admire and display, but also as an investment. The quiz that follows is on artists and their metier.

1. He failed at West Point, mainly because of chemistry. Later in life, after becoming a successful painter, he remarked: "How strange is fate. If silicon had been a gas, then I would have been a General." Who was this man?

2. Somerset Maugham's novel *The Moon and Sixpence* was based on the life of which painter?

3. She was born in 1913 in Budapest to a Hungarian mother and a Sikh father. Her works, which gave a new light to Indian painting, are admired for their depth and innovative skills. Who was this artist, to whom goes the credit for modernizing art in India?

4. Which famous tapestry was made to celebrate the Norman Conquest of England in 1066?

5. The world may never have known this great artist due to a nearly fatal misjudgment at his birth. The midwife thought he was stillborn and abandoned him on a table. His uncle, a cigar smoking physician, however saved the day by reviving the baby with a blast of air into his lungs. Who was this lucky man?

6. Which member of the surrealist movement was expelled from the Academy of Fine Arts in Madrid in 1923?

7. Remembered above all for his sculptures and paintings, he was also one of the Renaissance period's finest architects and a talented poet. He was the first artist to have his biography published during his lifetime. Who was this man, thought of as one of the greatest geniuses in the history of art?

8. Which painter was born on Good Friday in 1483 and died on Good Friday in 1520?

9. He was one of the best early American portrait painters and would have been remembered as a painter, had he not devised a famous code named after him. Can you figure out who he was?

10. This French painter won 100,000 francs in the state lottery in 1891. With this newfound financial independence, he could do what he wanted to, and wandered about painting the French countryside. He experimented with painting outside, which was a new idea at the time. In 1874, he helped organize an exhibition at which he showcased his picture *Impression: Sunrise*. It was this painting that gave the Impressionist movement its name, and he became one of its leading members. Who was he?

11. This method of producing colored designs on textiles by applying wax to the parts to be left uncolored was originally used in Java and derives its name from the Malay word for "war painting." What is it?

12. As a young man, he had several jobs, none of which satisfied him. Eventually, he joined a missionary society and began preaching to coal miners in Belgium, but was dismissed and spent the next few years living in great poverty. He began painting the vegetation and countryside around the town of Arles, where he lived. Troubled by bouts of depression and anxiety, he even cut off his ear in 1889 after a quarrel with Gauguin. The

following year, he shot himself in the cornfield which had been the subject of his last painting *Cornfield with Flight of Birds*? Who was this temperamental artist?

13. What is the claim to fame of Henri Matisse's *Le Bateau*, which was exhibited in New York's Museum of Modern Art in 1961?

14. Which painting would you find on the wall of the refectory of Santa Maria delle Grazie in Milan?

Answers

1. James McNeil Whistler.

2. Paul Gauguin.

3. Amrita Shergill.

4. The Bayeux Tapestry.

5. Pablo Picasso.

6. Salvador Dali.

7. Michelangelo Buanarotti.

8. Raphael.

9. Samuel Morse, who invented the Morse code.

10. Claude Monet.

11. Batik.

12. Vincent Van Gogh.

13.   This was the painting that was shown for forty-seven days before a visitor noticed it was upside down. More than 100,000 people had seen it before the mistake was noted!

14.   Leonardo da Vinci's *The Last Supper*.

Men of Letters

While accepting the Nobel Prize for Literature in 1962, John Steinbeck said: "The ancient commission of the author has not changed. He is charged with exposing our many grievous faults and failures, with dredging up to the light of our dark and dangerous dreams for the purpose of improvement. Furthermore, the writer is delegated to declare and to celebrate man's proven capacity for greatness of heart and spirit—for gallantry in defeat—for courage, compassion and love." That about sums up the work of the people on whom the quiz that follows is based.

1.   With no previous experience as an author, he wrote and sold his first novel—*A Princess of Mars*—in 1912. In the ensuing thirty-eight years until his death in 1950, he wrote ninety-one books and a host of short stories. His prolific pen ranged from the American West to primitive Africa and on to romantic adventures on the moon, the planets and even beyond the furthest star. However, he is remembered for a certain character he created. Whom are we talking about?

2.   He was born in 1920 in Luton, England, where he attended school, then worked as an office boy and clerk. Aged 19 at the outbreak of World War II, he joined the Royal Air Force to become a pilot. In 1947, he emigrated to Canada where he was successively a real-estate salesman, business magazine editor and a sales executive, before becoming a full-time author in 1956 following the overnight success of his television play *Flight Into Danger*. Who is he?

3.   He was a well-known screenwriter who wrote the screenplay for
        The Great Escape and *To Sir With Love,* which he also directed
        and produced. However, he is better known to us as an author
        of some epic novels. Who?

4.   In 1977, he wrote a book called *Our Struggle,* in which he
        exhorted the Arabs to unite to divide the western nations, using
        their dependence on Arab oil. Whom are we talking about?

5.   This playwright was expelled from Princeton University for
        throwing a beer bottle through the college President's window.
        He later became Charlie Chaplin's father-in-law. Who was he?

6.   Apart from all being authors, what is common to Arthur Conan
        Doyle, Somerset Maugham, AJ Cronin and Anton Chekhov?

7.   In 1973, this author charged $50 a couple to attend his 50th
        birthday celebrations, the money to go towards establishing a
        democratic secret police. Who was he?

8.   Which curious writer wrote his magazine articles on pink paper,
        poetry on yellow and novels on blue paper?

9.   He was born in Russia near Smolensk in 1920 and brought to
        the United States by his parents three years later. Prolific by any
        standards, he wrote highly successful detective mystery stories, a
        four volume *Guide to the Bible,* a biographical dictionary, ency-
        clopaedias, textbooks, books on many aspects of science, as well
        as two volumes of an autobiography. Nevertheless, it was his
        writing in a particular genre that won him worldwide fame and
        critical acclaim. Who was this eclectic writer?

10.   He was an American by birth, left for Europe very early in his
        life and spent most of his literary life there. Along with Yeats, he
        championed Tagore's cause in Britain. He broadcast for the Axis

powers from Rome during World War II and was saved from standing trial after the war only because of his poor health. Who was he?

11.   This novelist's first books were inspired by his experiences as an army officer during the Crimean war. At the end of it, he traveled around Europe before marrying and returning to his family estates in his country. He was a liberal landlord who introduced modern farming methods and built schools and proper homes for the people who lived and worked on his land. Can you guess who he was?

12.   Spurned by publisher after publisher in England, this disheartened author asked a friend to dump the manuscript of his book into the River Thames. Instead, his friend passed it on to Graham Greene, who was delighted with it, gave it a name and helped to get it published. Who was the author and what was the book?

13.   George Orwell wrote *1984*. Who wrote *1985*?

Answers

1.   Edgar Rice Burroughs, the creator of Tarzan.

2.   Arthur Hailey.

3.   James Clavell, author of books like Tai-Pan and Shogun.

4.   Saddam Hussein! If only George Bush had known…

5.   Eugene O'Neill. Incidentally, the college President was a man who went on to become the President of the United States–Woodrow Wilson.

6.   They were all qualified doctors.

7.   Norman Mailer.

8.   Alexandre Dumas.

9.   Isaac Asimov, arguably the greatest science-fiction writer ever.

10.   Ezra Pound.

11.   Leo Tolstoy.

12.   R. K. Narayan and *Swamy and his Friends*.

13.   Anthony Burgess.

Going Places

The quiz that follows is on places all over the world, mostly well known cities. You don't have to be well traveled to tackle it, though it might help!

1. A major part of London was destroyed in the Great Fire of London. A large part of the rubble was used to build a part of another great city. Which one?

2. The explorer who discovered this place gave it a name that would give his countrymen the impression that the place was very fertile and suitable for settlement. In reality, however, it is mostly barren. Which place is this?

3. Which city's name means "City of brotherly love"?

4. This city is so called because French sailors who first saw the rocky promontory cried: "What a beak!" Which city are we referring to?

5. It was purchased by Peter Minuit for 60 guilders. Today, it would be impossible to determine its value. What is it?

6. This city's name is the transcription of the local pronunciation of the Peking dialect version of "*Xiang gang*" meaning "a port of incense." Which city are we talking about?

7. This place in South India is known for its flourishing coir industry and the annual snake-boat race held in the nearby backwaters. Which place is this, often referred to as the Venice of the East?

8. Which is the largest landlocked country in the world? This question isn't as easy as it sounds.

9. In 1590, Portuguese traders on sighting an island shouted, "Beautiful Island, Beautiful Island" (in Portuguese) thus giving it its name. Which island was this?

10. Marinus, a Christian stonecutter fleeing from the Roman emperor Diocletian, is said to have founded this European country in the 4th century AD. Can you guess which country this is?

11. In 1642, a Dutch navigator discovered an island and named it *Van Dieman's Land* in honor of the Dutch Governor of the East Indies. It was later renamed after its discoverer? Do you know which island this is?

12. Which European nation has as its joint Heads of State, the Bishop of the Spanish town of La Seu d'Urgell and the President of France?

13. What is the claim to fame of Deolpur, a sleepy rural hamlet a few hours from Calcutta?

Answers

1. St. Petersburg.

2. Greenland, which is hardly green.

3. Philadelphia.

4. Quebec, from the French "*Quel bec!*"

5. Manhattan.

6.   Hong Kong.

7.   Allepey.

8.   You've probably been brought up to believe it's Mongolia, and until a few years ago, you would have been right. But after the break-up of the Soviet Union, the correct answer is Kazakhstan. A point to note is that Kazakhstan does border the Caspian Sea, which is really only a lake, since it is totally surrounded by land.

9.   Formosa (now Taiwan). The sailors shouted, "*Ilha Formosa, Ilha Formosa.*"

10.   San Marino.

11.   Tasmania, named after Abel Tasman.

12.   Andorra.

13.   It is the only place in the world where wooden polo balls are made.

In Good Company

This section is on the firms, individuals and concepts that comprise the business world–the movers and shakers of the corporate whirl.

1. In 1955, a 52-year-old businessman named Ray Kroc bought a chain of seven restaurants for $2.7 million along with its name. He assiduously developed it, and today it is one of the most powerful brand-names in the world. Which restaurant chain are we talking about?

2. The launch of this "product" code-named Chicago, was much delayed, causing a competitor to release advertisements saying: "Flight 4.0 to Chicago is delayed." What was it?

3. What are widow's shares?

4. Who is the author of the book *Le Piege (The Trap)*, filled with dire warnings against huge transnational corporations and the breakdown of social order?

5. A New York businessman named Frank McNamara once discovered to his embarrassment that he did not have enough money to pay the bill at a restaurant. What did this inspire him to start in 1950?

6. Whose autobiography begins (with the first two words deleted): "my father arrived in this country in 1902 at the age of twelve–poor, alone and scared. He used to say that the only thing he was sure of when he got here was that the world was round. And that was only because another Italian boy named

Christopher Columbus had preceded him by 410 years, almost to the day"?

7. When Polaroid introduced its cameras in Russia, sales were unusually good despite the high price. Research showed that this was due to an unanticipated reason. What?

8. In the early part of the last century, Marcus Samuel opened a shop in London that sold objects made of shells. Other items were slowly added, and today it is one of the largest corporations in the world. Which company is this?

9. When the founders of Hewlett-Packard, William Hewlett and David Packard, produced their first commercial audio oscillator, they named it Model 200A to make it sound as if they had been in business for a while. Whimsically, they priced it at $54.40. Why?

10. In business, what is the Pac-man strategy?

11. The increase in the price of a pound of pepper by five shillings, proclaimed by the Dutch privateers who controlled the spice trade, incensed twenty-four merchants of London. The merchants gathered together on the afternoon of September 24, 1599 in a decrepit building on Leadenhall Street, to found a modest trading firm with an initial capital of 72,000 pounds, subscribed by 125 shareholders. Which organization thus came into existence?

12. Which management concept was developed by Taichi Ohno of Toyota, who compared the movement of automobile components at Toyota factories with that of consumer goods in American supermarkets?

13.   In the financial world, what are bonds maturing in 2007 collo-
        quially referred to as?

Answers

1.   McDonald's.

2.   Windows '95.

3.   Shares of fundamentally strong companies, which can be bought
        and forgotten about as they are very safe. The term was coined
        because widows who had no exposure to the world of finance,
        could with their eyes closed, buy these shares and sleep easy.

4.   The corporate raider and billionaire James Goldsmith. Talk of
        hypocrisy! Goldsmith is perhaps better known to us as Imran
        Khan's father-in-law. Incidentally, Imran translated this book
        into Urdu.

5.   Diners Club, the world's first credit card. For decades, this
        story was recounted as the inspiration behind the creation of
        our cashless society. Unfortunately, it was revealed as a hoax
        in a 1995 book *The Credit Card Catastrophe*, written by Matty
        Simmons. Simmons, Diners Club's first publicity manager,
        said that he fabricated the incident to "glamorize"
        McNamara's effort.

6.   Lee Iacocca, who rejuvenated Chrysler.

7.   Since the person got the photographs immediately and didn't
        need to give the negatives for developing, the KGB could not
        obtain them clandestinely!

8.   Shell.

9.   After "Fifty four forty or fight"–a slogan used in establishing the
       US border in the Pacific North West (54° 40'). Luckily, their
       nearest competitor was selling oscillators at $400!

10.   You gobble up the company that's trying to gobble you.

11.   The East India Company.

12.   Benchmarking.

13.   James Bonds!

Comic Opera

Cartoons and comics have been a perennial favorite of both young and old. This quiz takes you on a trip into the world of fantasy and make-believe, which can be as interesting as it is entertaining.

1. America's first comic strip was Richard F. Outcault's *Yellow Kid*, published in 1896. It was about a sassy, aged baby on whose sack-like yellow garment were printed words that he presumably spoke or thought. His pithy earthiness made him extremely popular, resulting in various newspapers vying for the privilege of printing this strip. This competitive spirit along with its accompanying bids and counter-bids gave rise to a certain term. What was it?

2. Who first made his appearance on June 9, 1934 in *The Wise Little Hen* with the words: "Who me? Oh no! I've got a belly-ache"?

3. This comic character was inspired by an unusual combination of sources–Leonardo da Vinci's notebook sketch of the *Ornithopter* glider, the silent-film version of a masked hero in *The Mark of Zorro* and the 1931 film version of the mystery novel *The Bat Whisper*. He first appeared in the May 1939 issue of *Detective Comics*. Whom are we talking about?

4. How do we better know Peter Parker?

5. What is common to Donatello, Michaelangelo, Leonardo and Raphael?

6. What was Operation Ulysses?

7. In the film *It Happened One Night*, Clark Gable is shown eating a carrot in one scene. This inspired Bob Clampett to create which cartoon character?

8. Why was Clark Kent (Superman) not drafted into the army in World War II?

9. Who are the founders of the organization GROSS (Get rid of slimy girls)?

10. The *Peanuts* character Linus' obsession with a blanket introduced which term into the English language?

11. Connect Hagar the Horrible with Shakespeare.

12. Popeye's girlfriend would make a good salad dressing. What is she called?

13. For this animated film, Walt Disney was presented one large Oscar and seven little ones by the then child actress Shirley Temple. Which film was this?

14. In *Asterix and the Magic Carpet*, a fakir brings Asterix to India. What's his name?

Answers

1. Yellow journalism.

2. Donald Duck.

3. Batman.

4. Spiderman.

5. They are the Ninja turtles.

6. Tintin's trip to the moon.

7. Bugs Bunny.

8. In the medical test, when he looked at the eye-chart, his x-ray vision made him see the chart in the next room. So he failed due to poor vision!

9. Calvin and Hobbes.

10. Security blanket.

11. Hagar's son is named Hamlet.

12. Olive Oyl.

13. What else but *Snow White and the Seven Dwarfs*.

14. Whatzisnehm!

Quotable Quotes

It was Benjamin Disraeli who said: "The wisdom of the wise and the experience of the ages are perpetuated by quotations." Though actions may speak louder than words, people have sometimes come up with words of enduring value.

1. Who is credited with the statement: "An archaeologist is the best husband a woman can get. The older she gets, the more interested he becomes"?

2. During the Normandy invasion, who inspired his troops saying, "Come on chaps, it's all right for you, but I shall have to go through all this again with Errol Flynn"?

3. The motto of the US state of Virginia is *Sic semper tyrannis*. Who uttered these same words while performing a heinous act?

4. Of whom did Hitler say, "He seemed such a nice gentleman, so I thought I'd give him my autograph"?

5. "It is only given to God and angels to fly." Who uttered these not too prophetic words?

6. "My slow ones are faster than the fast ones of others." Who made this perhaps justifiable boast?

7. Inviting him to lead his company, who wrote to whom: "Do you want to spend the rest of your life selling sugared water, or do you want a chance to change the world?"

8. Who said to whom: "I thank God I've been permitted to see you"?

9.   He had a pay-phone installed in his English country house because he hated to pay for his guests' calls. This, when he was rich enough to comment: "If you can count your millions, you are not a billionaire." Who was he?

10. Who or what was Ebenezer Elliot describing in the early 19th century by the epigram, "One who hath yearnings for equal division of unequal earnings"?

11. Which author and playwright once said: "I can forgive Nobel for having invented dynamite, but only a fiend in human form could have invented the Nobel Prize"?

12. Who said about whom: "I've seen him shadow boxing, and the shadow invariably won"?

13. Who commented facetiously: "You know why Brooke Shields refused to marry me? Because if she did, she would have been Brooke Bond!"

Answers

1.   Agatha Christie, who was married to the archaeologist Sir Max Mallowan.

2.   The actor David Niven.

3.   John Booth while assassinating Abraham Lincoln.

4.   Neville Chamberlain, the British Prime Minister, after signing the Munich Pact with him.

5.   Bishop Wright, father of Orville and Wilbur Wright, who invented the airplane.

6.   Edwin Moses, at one time the undisputed king of the 400 meters hurdles.

7.   Steve Jobs to John Sculley, then with Pepsi, asking him to move to Apple Computers. Incidentally, the only thing Sculley did to come close to changing the world, was to throw Jobs out of the company the latter had founded!

8.   Henry Morton Stanley to Dr. David Livingstone. These were his words after the famous "Dr. Livingstone, I presume?"

9.   Jean Paul Getty, Jr.

10.   A communist.

11.   George Bernard Shaw.

12.   Muhammad Ali about George Foreman.

13.   Ruskin Bond.

The Living World

This set of questions is on the plants and animals with whom we share our planet. Test your knowledge about the flora and fauna around us by going through it.

1. In the 4th century BC, Aristotle helped pioneer the systematic study of animals. He persuaded a former student of his to provide him with living samples of unfamiliar species. Who was this student?

2. The wood of which tree was used to make Christ's cross?

3. This animal can produce two different kinds of milk at the same time from adjacent teats to feed both younger and older offspring. Which peculiar creature is this?

4. What is General Sherman in the record books for?

5. Europeans originally thought this animal was a cross between a camel and a leopard and hence called it a "camelopard." We now know better. What do we call it today?

6. What did Ralph Waldo Emerson describe as "a plant whose virtues have not yet been discovered"?

7. What is peculiar about the Basenji, a dog of African breed?

8. This African animal has a head resembling that of a giraffe and a body like a zebra's, with a chestnut coat and black-and-white stripes on the hind-quarters and upper legs only. It has a fourteen inch long tongue with which it cleans its face and even its ears. What is this unusual animal?

9.   This evergreen tree, whose scientific name is *Camellia sinensis*, grows to a height of about thirty feet in nature. What do we get from it?

10.   Why do geese fly in a V-formation while migrating?

11.   In fable, this plant was thought to shriek when plucked from the ground, because its forked root resembles the human form. Which "magic" plant is this?

12.   What was the Malay term for the savage people of the Sunda Islands, which literally means "man-of-the-woods"? It is now applied to an animal, though.

13.   If this tree were to become extinct, the koala bear would be wiped off the face of this earth too, since its diet consists solely of the leaves of this tree. Which tree are we referring to?

14.   This flowering plant was considered so valuable in seventeenth century Amsterdam that collectors paid incredible sums for prize specimens. It even caused the first boom and slump in capitalism's history and when its market crashed in 1637, it shook the Dutch economy. Can you guess which plant this was?

15.   To round off, do you know which is the longest living mammal in the world?

Answers

1.   Alexander the Great. Since he went on to conquer much of the known world, the collection of animals was impressive indeed!

2.   Aspen.

3.   Red kangaroo.

4.   It is the largest tree in the world, a sequoia pine in California, USA.

5.   Giraffe.

6.   A weed.

7.   It is the only dog that doesn't bark.

8.   Okapi.

9.   Tea. Under cultivation, it is pruned to a bush-like 3-5 feet.

10.   It's actually efficient energy management. The leader stirs up air, enabling the following geese to fly in its wake, expending the minimum possible amount of energy. In true democratic tradition, the geese take turns being the leader.

11.   Mandrake.

12.   Orangutan.

13.   Eucalyptus.

14.   Tulip.

15.   Man.

Who is it?

This quiz is on an assortment of people, the only thing connecting them being the fact that they are remembered for something or the other. However, an attempt is made to present facts about them that are interesting, but obscure and not well known.

1. He is the only Westerner to be awarded the Order of Lenin and hates the *Beatles*. He once said that drinking Dom Perignon champagne before it has chilled sufficiently would be like listening to the *Beatles* without ear-muffs. His pseudonyms include David Somerset, James Stock and Robert Stirling. Who is he?

2. When this person received an honorary degree from Yale University, it was said of him: "He has accomplished something that has defied all the efforts and experiments of the laboratories in zoology and biology. He has given animals souls." Who is it?

3. She was the daughter of Powhatan, an Indian chief of Virginia, and was the first Native American to be baptized. She was said to have rescued Captain John Smith when her father was on the point of killing him. She subsequently married Sir John Rolfe, the first Englishman to plant and cure tobacco. Who was this woman?

4. He was half French and half Indian. His father was a Paris based pearl and silk merchant. He never had a college education, but was immensely successful in life. Can you guess who he was?

5.   She is a graduate of Wellesley and Yale Law School and was a
       senior partner in a major American law firm. Twice named one
       of the top 100 lawyers in the US, she is known for her legal
       scholarship and her activism in the field of children's rights.
       Whom are we referring to?

6.   He was a many-sided genius who won eminence in the fields of
       mathematics, philosophy and literature. In addition, he found
       time to run a large insurance company, advise the British treas-
       ury, help govern the Bank of England, edit a world-famous eco-
       nomics journal, collect modern art and rare books, and sponsor
       ballet and drama. He was also an economist who knew how to
       make money by shrewd speculation, both for himself and for
       King's College, Cambridge. Who was this distinguished figure?

7.   Born in 1779, he trained as a doctor and practised medicine in
       London from 1808 to 1840. In 1824, he wrote *The Persistence of
       Vision with Regard to Moving Objects*–a document setting out the
       principle that the eye retains an image of the continuation of
       movement for a time after the stimulus of watching a body in
       motion. This resulted in a variety of devices that were the
       forerunners of the motion-picture projector: the Zoetrope, the
       Stroboscope and the Praxinoscope. Who was this man,
       remembered for something else he did?

8.   In June 1987, he tried to buy the remains of John Merrick, the
       "Elephant Man" of Victorian times, whose tragic outcast life he
       believed to be similar in many ways to his own. He offered the
       London Medical College $1 million for the bones of Merrick,
       who had died in 1900. Who is he?

9.   His father Fred, a ship's waiter, set sail before he was born and
       never returned to take responsibility of his wife and child. His
       mother Julia waited for three years and then left him with her

elder sister Mimi, to live with another man. Caught between two contrasting mother figures, his insecurity and confusion soon turned him into a rebellious, arrogant and vitriolic gang leader by the time he was in his teens. Whom are we talking about?

10. He lives behind closed blinds in Pasadena, California, in fear that the Russians will kidnap or assassinate him. When he does venture out, he adopts disguises and uses the name Robert D James. He is believed to have given most of his money to the Worldwide Church of God, a religious sect that believes Satan is in charge of the world, running governments. Who is this reclusive figure?

Answers

1. His name is Bond–James Bond.

2. Walt Disney.

3. Pocahontas, made famous by the Hollywood film on her.

4. J. R. D. Tata.

5. Hillary Clinton.

6. John Maynard Keynes. His 1936 book *The General Theory of Employment, Interest and Money* presented a challenge to then macroeconomic thinking and provided the groundwork for modern mainstream macroeconomics.

7. Peter Mark Roget, better known for the thesaurus he compiled.

8. Michael Jackson.

9.   John Lennon.

10.   Bobby Fischer.

Games People Play

All work and no play makes Jack a dull boy. Hence, this section on a few of the people and games in the sporting world.

1. He was born in Brooklyn on January 30, 1966 and never knew who his father was. He became a ruffian and joined a gang called *Jolly Stompers*. On his right biceps is a tattooed portrait of Mao Tse-tung and on the left that of Arthur Ashe. Who is this controversial sportsman?

2. At the YMCA Training School in Springfield, Massachusetts, the students of an instructor named James Naismith complained that they found the daily gymnasium classes boring. In response to this, Naismith invented a fast-paced game using two peach baskets and a soccer ball. Which game was this, which is now a major sport in the United States and the world?

3. How many Wimbledon singles titles has Ivan Lendl won?

4. When Gary Sobers played the role of a cricketer in the film *Two Gentlemen Sharing*, he imposed two conditions. One was that he would not wear any make-up. What was the other?

5. Who owns a private jet with the call sign N-792 AA to represent his first grand Slam title at Wimbledon in July 1992?

6. A star in the Lepus constellation is named after an Argentinean soccer player, an honor for which his fans paid $200. Who is he?

7. This game is thought to have originated in India as *Poona*. It was brought to England in 1873, where it took its present name

through association with the seat of the Duke of Beaufort in Avon. Which game is this?

8. The George Foreman-Muhammad Ali heavyweight boxing title fight in 1974 in Kinshasa, Zaire started at 4 a.m. Why was it scheduled to begin at so early an hour?

9. Which sport did Oscar Wilde refer to as "the unspeakable in pursuit of the uneatable"?

10. What is the contribution of Christina Wells to the game of cricket?

11. This sports personality has lent his name to a range of cologne that includes the grassy smell of a golf course, a hint of pine to evoke his home in North Carolina, and a leather scent to recall his two year stint in minor league baseball. The bottle has a suggested retail price of $23 to match his shirt number. Who is he?

12. William Webb Ellis committed a foul in a soccer match in 1839. What did this lead to?

13. What is the winner of the Indy (Indianapolis) 500 car race toasted with?

14. This versatile sportswoman captained the English hockey team, got a silver medal in archery in the 1908 Olympics, and won the British golf championship. To top it all, she won five Wimbledon titles. Who was she?

15. Arthur Conan Doyle, apart from being an eminent author, was also a cricketer of some note, and even took a wicket in a first-class game. Whom did he dismiss?

16. He is a founder of the Democratic Party of Russia, a computer expert, a successful businessman, and the youngest ever contributing editor to the *Wall Street Journal*. Who is he?

17. Many Japanese golfers carry hole-in-one insurance. What is it for?

Answers

1. Mike Tyson.

2. Basketball.

3. One, and not zero as is commonly believed. Lendl won the Boys' Singles Championship at Wimbledon in 1978 when he was eighteen years old.

4. That a real fast bowler would bowl at him.

5. Andre Agassi.

6. Gabriel Batistuta.

7. Badminton, from Badminton Hall.

8. It was designed to accommodate millions of Americans watching the bout live on closed circuit television.

9. Fox hunting.

10. She pioneered the use of over-arm bowling! Until then, under-arm bowling was the norm, but she found that her skirt came in the way when she performed the necessary action. So she started bowling over-arm and it soon caught on.

11. Michael Jordan.

12. The creation of the game of rugby.

13.   Milk.

14.   Lottie Dod.

15.   The great W. G. Grace.

16.   Gary Kasparov.

17.   It is traditional in Japan to share one's good luck by sending gifts
       to all one's friends on hitting a hole-in-one. To defray the
       expense involved, Japanese golfers get insurance!

Scientific Sense

Science and scientists have done more to advance our civilization than arguably anything else. It is thus only appropriate that we pay a tribute to science and those who dedicated their lives to it, through this quiz.

1. The main early publication on the creation of heavier elements in the Big Bang was by Ralph Alpher, Hans Bethe and George Gamow, although the work was done by only Alpher and Gamow. Why did Bethe get credit for work he did not do?

2. In 1749, the French scientist Abbe Jean Antoine Nollet wanted to find out how fast electricity traveled. What did he do to help him discover this?

3. When this scientist was born, his mother performed a curious ritual. She had him carried to the top of the house in the belief that this would help him rise to the top of his profession when he grew up. The same ambitious mother was to reassure her son, who as a science-crazed school-boy despaired that everything in science would have been discovered by the time he grew up. "Don't worry Ducky," she told him. "There will be plenty left for you to find." And indeed there was. Who was this anxious scientist?

4. What common irritation is produced by the chemical *propane-thiol-s-oxide*?

5. This new computer language developed by James Gosling, is designed for network computing and is totally machine

independent and can run on any computer or digital device. What is it?

6.   William Shockley, one of the inventors of the transistor, had a penchant for bizarre terminology. He introduced what is a powerful analytical tool in semiconductor device physics–the IMREF level. The term itself, however, was suggested by another scientist. Who?

7.   Vitamins were originally called vitamines. Why was the final "e" dropped?

8.   The most prominent astronomer of the late 16th century, he was an extraordinarily quarrelsome and arrogant man. Over a point in mathematics, he engaged in a midnight duel that cost him his nose when he was nineteen years old in 1565. Who was this man, who for the rest of his life wore a false nose of metal?

9.   The names of four elements are derived from the name of this place in Sweden. Which place is this?

10.   He was a son of a blacksmith and a book-binder's apprentice and satiated his fascination for science by studying at night. Since he had no academic credentials to present to the master he had chosen for himself, he sent the volume of notes he had taken while attending the latter's lectures. He was accepted as a bottle washer. Who was this boy who went on to become a great inventor?

11.   He was born on the 300th anniversary of Galileo's death. At 21, he developed amyotrophic lateral sclerosis(ALS), a disorder that has rendered him paralyzed and incapable of performing most kinds of work. He is the Lucasian professor of mathematics at Cambridge–a post once held by Isaac Newton. Who is this person, considered by some to be the greatest theoretical physicist

since Einstein, but owes his stardom to a best-selling book that he wrote?

12. What is technically termed "pilomotor response"?

13. As a member of the British Parliament, his only words were a request for a window to be opened. He had a more successful stint as a Master of the Mint, during which he recalled old currency and substituted them with circularly milled coins, making counterfeiting difficult. Who was this great scientist, who had a dog named Diamond?

Answers

1. It occurred to Gamow that the names Alpher and Gamow sounded almost like *alpha* and *gamma*, so he invited the eminent physicist Bethe (whose name exactly fit the missing *beta*) to join them in signing the paper!

2. He arranged two hundred Carthusian monks in a large circle, wired them together and sent a stiff charge through the wire. He learnt that electricity traveled very fast indeed!

3. Francis Crick, who along with James Watson discovered the double helix structure of DNA.

4. Watering of eyes while cutting onions.

5. Java.

6. Enrico Fermi. IMREF is Fermi spelt backwards.

7. The American biochemist Casimir Funk, who coined the word in 1912, believed that they were essential to sustain life–hence *vita*–and belonged to the *amine* group of

chemicals. He was quickly proved wrong on the second count, and the "e" was duly dropped!

8.   Tycho Brahe.

9.   Ytterby. The elements are Ytterbium, Yttrium, Terbium and Erbium.

10.   Michael Faraday. His master was another eminent scientist, Humphrey Davy.

11.   Stephen Hawking, the author of *A Brief History of Time*.

12.   Body hair standing up.

13.   Isaac Newton.

Times Gone by

"Those who do not remember the past are condemned to repeat it," said the philosopher George Santayana. So let us not forget the past, but rather refresh our memories with this brief travel through time.

1. In Julius Caesar's time, it was not lawful for a private citizen to stamp his name on public money. When he was Master of the Roman Mint, how did Caesar get around this rule to leave a personal mark on Roman money?

2. When Martin Waldseemueller, a cartographer in the Middle Ages was updating "the most respected geography text of the day" and the time came to name a certain area, he decided to designate it after an explorer who had gone there and sent back titillating reports laced with wild adventures, bizarre events and lewd encounters. What name did he give the region?

3. The Maharajahs of Jaipur in India used to bear the hereditary title of *Sawai,* meaning one-and-a-quarter. This honor was bestowed by the Emperor Aurangzeb. Why?

4. Which tragic event was triggered off during the siege of Caffa, a Crimean port held by Genoese traders, by a Kipchak (Tartar) army in the 14th century?

5. What was sold to France in 1768, just in time to make one of its citizens perhaps the greatest Frenchman ever?

6. Its first stones were laid in the late 12th century under King Philip Augustus, who constructed it as a fortress to protect Paris while he led a crusade to the Holy Land. It was converted to a

royal palace in the 14th century and inhabited by the French monarch, until Louis XIV abandoned it for the splendor of Versailles in the 17th century. However, it continued to grow and change until the late 19th century, when it finally settled into its present U-shape. What are we talking about?

7.   What is the significance of the play *Our American Cousin* in the history of the United States?

8.   In the days of the Raj in India, what would a judge do after passing a death sentence?

9.   For many centuries, scholars in Europe believed that women had only thirty teeth, compared to the thirty-two men had. Why?

10.   What is common to the Battle of Belle Alliance and the Battle of Mont St. Jean?

11.   This Greek excelled as a soldier and twice won prizes at the Isthmian games. He was given his name, it is said, because of the breadth of his shoulders. Who was he?

Answers

1.   In the Punic language, "Caesar" signified an elephant. So Caesar put an elephant on the reverse of the coins!

2.   America, after Amerigo Vespucci.

3.   Aurangzeb was so impressed by the wit of the then Maharajah of Jaipur, that he bestowed this title to denote that the latter's family was 25 per cent smarter than the rest of humanity.

4.   The Black Death, the outbreak of bubonic plague in Europe, that caused the death of more than a quarter of the population.

During the siege, some of the Tartar soldiers who had brought the disease from Central Asia, caused an outbreak among the Tartar army. They catapulted the dead bodies into the town, and soon its inhabitants were down with the disease. Later, it spread all over Europe.

5.   Corsica. The person concerned was Napoleon Bonaparte.

6.   The Louvre.

7.   It was the play which Abraham Lincoln was watching when he was assassinated.

8.   He broke the nib of his fountain pen.

9.   Because Aristotle had said so. It never occurred to them that they only had to make their wives open their mouths and count, to find out that this wasn't true!

10.   Both are names used to refer to what we better know as the Battle of Waterloo. It is given the former name in German reference works and the latter in French encyclopaedias. Incidentally, Waterloo was actually some distance away from the scene of action. It was called the Battle of Waterloo because the Duke of Wellington, Arthur Wellesley, liked to name his battles after the place where he had spent the previous night!

11.   Plato.

What's the Good Word?

Words often have colorful origins, which serve as insights into the past. See if you can identify these words with the help of the clues given below.

1. For starters, which word is derived from the first two letters of the Greek alphabet?

2. The Mongol word for "Ocean" is used as an honorific title. What is it?

3. The Finance Minister of France just before the French revolution, instituted a wave of new taxes in the hope of restoring the economy. However, this led to a further deterioration in the economy and he was forced to resign after eight months. His name soon became associated with cheap and "empty" commodities, such as pocketless trousers and shadow portraits. Who was he?

4. What cabalistic charm word is made up from the initials of the Hebrew words for Father, Son and Holy Spirit?

5. Which word was coined by William Gibson in 1984 in his novel *Neuromancer*?

6. The name of the land agent, who was hired by the Earl of Earne to collect high rents from his impoverished Irish tenants, has entered the English language. What was his name?

7.   Which word entered the English language as a result of the estrangement between the actor Lee Marvin and his live-in girl-friend Michelle Triola?

8.   This famous character in Sheridan's *The Rivals* was noted for blunders in the use of words and has hence lent her name to a word denoting such mistakes. Who was she?

9.   In the medieval days, a checkered cloth was used for calculations regarding the English Crown's income and expenditure. What word did this give rise to?

10.   This word emanates from the Latin word for "cow," because what it refers to was first derived from a cow. Which word is it?

11.   Which Russian word was absorbed into English to describe out-bursts against Jews, which occurred between 1881 and 1914?

12.   Which English word is derived from the Hindu God Jagannath, whose idol is carried in a procession on a huge cart, under which devotees used to throw themselves?

13.   This person was an officer during the time of the American Revolution and was known for summary executions without trial of lawless Tories and desperadoes. What word did he con-tribute to the English language?

14.   Which word is derived from the Greek word for "pebble" because the Greek method of voting was to cast a pebble into "yes" or "no" urns?

15.   In ancient Rome, a person who solicited public office always wore a loose white robe. The Latin word for "clothed in white" has hence given rise to an English word. Which one?

Answers

1. Alphabet itself, from alpha and beta.

2. Dalai, as in Dalai Lama.

3. Etienne de Silhouette.

4. Abracadabra.

5. Cyberspace.

6. Charles Boycott.

7. Palimony.

8. Mrs. Malaprop.

9. Exchequer.

10. Vaccine from *vacca*.

11. Pogrom.

12. Juggernaut.

13. Lynch. He was Col. Charles Lynch.

14. Psephology, from psephos.

15. Candidate.

Something New

The curiosity of man about the things around him, and his constant attempts to improve on the status quo, have led to the application of ingenuity to make newer and better things. Go through the next few pages and learn that necessity is not always the mother of invention.

1. While working as a newsboy and candy salesman on the railroad between Port Huron and Michigan, Ohio, he installed a second-hand printing press on which he produced a weekly newspaper, the *Grand Trunk Herald*, for sale on the train. Who was this man, who went on to become a great inventor?

2. A small electronic device called *Cyclops*, invented in Malta in 1978 by a local woman named Margaret Parnis England and a British engineer named Bill Carlton, is now widely used in a particular sport. What is the function of this device?

3. It was "invented" by George Nichols, a project manager for Northrop, the Californian aviation firm, in 1949. He developed the idea from a remark made by a colleague at the Wright Field Aircraft Laboratory. What is it? Hint: It was a prescription for avoiding mistakes in the design of a valve for an aircraft's hydraulic system.

4. Its inventor conceived it while studying sitar music in an ashram in India and said with respect to it: "Real high fidelity means reproducing the silence as accurately as the sound." What are we talking about?

5.   In the 1860s in America, a prize of $10,000 was put up for any-
        one who could find a cheap replacement for ivory billiard balls.
        What invention did this lead to?

6.   In 1830, Edwin Budding of England invented a machine for
        finishing heavy woolen cloth. However, it could not be used in
        the mills because of opposition from the Luddites (who were
        destroying machines). So what did Budding turn his
        invention into?

7.   It was invented in 1824 by an Englishman named John Aspdin,
        who burned limestone and clay together and ground the mix-
        ture into a fine powder. What is it?

8.   Jack Ryan, the former husband of the actress Zsa Zsa Gabor,
        invented something that sells millions across the world today.
        What did he devise?

9.   He was a Scottish engineer, unkempt in appearance and
        notoriously absent-minded. After several unsuccessful business
        ventures such as making undersocks for cold feet, jam in Trinidad,
        soap, pneumatic shoes and glass razors, he finally invented
        something that has secured him a place amongst the great
        inventors. Who was he and what was his invention?

10.   On a voyage from England to the United States in 1832 on
        board the ship *Sully*, one of the passengers, Dr. Charles Thomas
        Jackson, a Boston physician, amused his fellow passengers with
        a simple act which provided the inspiration for a seminal inven-
        tion. Which one?

11.   What originated when Brazilian Indians stuck their feet into liq-
        uid latex and allowed it to harden?

Answers

1. Thomas Alva Edison.

2. It sets off a sound for a fault service in tennis.

3. Murphy's Law (If anything can go wrong, it will). If the valve could be fitted in more than one way, then sooner or later someone would fit it the wrong way. The idea was to design it so that the valve could only be fitted the right way.

4. Dolby stereo.

5. It led to the development of celluloid, the world's first synthetic plastic, by the winner John Wesley Hyatt.

6. The lawnmower.

7. Portland cement.

8. The Barbie doll.

9. John Logie Baird, who invented the television.

10. The Morse Code. Dr. Jackson had alternately energized and de-energized an electromagnet, making it first attract and then drop iron nails. This phenomenon, Samuel Morse realized, could be used to send messages over long distances. When he left the ship, he was even cocky enough to tell the Captain, "If you should one day hear of a new world wonder called the electric telegraph, remember that the discovery was made on board your ship."

11. Sneakers.

Mathematical Games

The subject of mathematics–bugbear of many a school and college student–has fascinated man since ancient times, and people have spent their lives studying and advancing it. It is often ignored in quizzes, but can be more interesting than you think, as this section based on the subject and its practitioners, will show you.

1. The mathematician M. G. Mittag-Leffler, whose work on complex theory is studied by every student today, has another claim to fame. What?

2. Which branch of mathematics derives its name from the fact that it formerly dealt only with affairs of state?

3. In 1619, in the military camp of the Duke of Bavaria, a soldier was lazily watching the movements of a fly. He attempted to describe its position, and this led him to propose a new mathematical concept. Who was this soldier and what was the concept?

4. The mathematician Cauchy once received a letter from a lesser mathematician positing that $x^3+y^3+z^3=T^3$ had no integral solutions. It was accompanied by a proof that ran to several pages. Cauchy sat down and patiently composed a one line reply. What was it?

5. Which branch of mathematics is based on an axiomatic approach developed by the famous Russian mathematician Kolmogoroff?

6. This mathematical concept was formulated when a French mathematician attempted to codify the number of soldiers dying of mule kicks in the Prussian army. Which one?

7.   He was the author of books like *The Fifth Book of Euclid Treated Algebraically, Condensation of Determinants* and *Curiosa Mathematica.* However, he is better known to us as the writer of vivid and imaginative books for children. Do you know who he was?

8.   Which sampling term was introduced during World War II as a code name for the simulation of problems associated with the development of the atomic bomb?

9.   The 18th century saw a battle between the d-ists and the dotters in Europe. What was it about?

10.   This 17th century French scientist, mathematician and philosopher was a precocious child who helped his father with experiments and calculations. He built a calculating machine and slide rule in his childhood, discovered the properties of the cycloid and worked on differential calculus. He also did important work on the effects of air pressure, which led to the invention of the barometer. In 1654, he suddenly joined his sister in a monastery where he began to defend certain Christian philosophies against the attacks of Jesuit thinkers. Who was he?

11.   Which mathematical concept emanated from the Polaris missile program of the United States defense department?

12.   An associate of Charles Babbage, she was an accomplished mathematician who developed the essential ideas of computer programming, which in their refined form are still valid today. She was also the daughter of a great literary figure. Can you guess who she was?

13.   This fictional character was endowed by nature with a phenomenal mathematical faculty. At the age of 21, he wrote a treatise on the binomial theorem. Who is he?

Answers

1. Alfred Nobel's wife eloped with him, and the absence of a Nobel Prize in mathematics is attributed to this!

2. Statistics.

3. Rene Descartes and the Cartesian coordinate system.

4. $3^3+4^3+5^3=6^3$.

5. The modern theory of probability.

6. The Poisson distribution. Although the probability of being kicked dead by a mule was very low, the sheer number of soldiers in contact with mules ensured that a good number of them did manage it!

7. C. L. Dodgson, better known as Lewis Carroll.

8. The Monte Carlo method.

9. The English scientist Isaac Newton and the German mathematician Gottfried Leibnitz had both independently developed the theory of calculus, and people were divided in their opinion as to who should get the credit. Mathematicians in Britain followed Newton's dot notation for differentiation, while in the rest of the continent, Leibnitz's method of using d (as in dy/dx) was preferred. Hence the conflict between the d-ists and the dotters.

10. Blaise Pascal.

11. PERT.

12.   Ada Lovelace, the daughter of Lord Byron.

13.   Professor Moriarty, from the *Sherlock Holmes* stories.

The Medium is the Message

The American humorist Will Rogers once said, "I hope we never live to see the day when a thing is as bad as some of our newspapers make it." Though the media may tend to sensationalize things occasionally, there is no doubt that they provide an invaluable service in today's world. Take this quiz and find out how much you know about the fourth estate.

1. Dramas on television are called soap operas. Can you guess why?

2. The Sunday supplement of the *New York Herald* carried something on December 21, 1913 that has since become a regular feature of most newspapers. What was it?

3. After the telecast of Princess Diana's BBC interview by Martin Bashir, in which she admitted to adultery, there was an upsurge in the demand for power, which the power companies had correctly anticipated and made plans to tackle. Why did this upsurge take place? Note that the upsurge was after, not during, the telecast.

4. This British media baron was born Jan Ludvik Hoch and died under mysterious circumstances aboard his yacht *Lady Ghislaine*. Who was he?

5. The news of Mahatma Gandhi's assassination was not carried on the front page of only one major Indian newspaper. Which one and why?

6. Are you one of those who starts smacking his/her lips at the sight of those mouth-watering ice-cream advertisements on

television? You might be disappointed to know that what you thought was delicious ice-cream isn't actually what it purports to be. Had they used real ice-cream, it would have long melted due to the heat from the lights used in the shooting, before they got the shot right. So what actually masquerades as ice-cream in those advertisements?

7.   Charles Dow and Edward Jones are best known for the New York share price index named after them. However, they also founded one of the world's leading dailies in 1889. Can you name it?

8.   What is unusual about the periodicity of publication of the French magazine *La Bougie du Sapeur*?

9.   In France it is *Alerte a Malibu*, in Venezuela *Guardianes de la Bahia* and in Hebrew it is called *Mishmar Ha-mifratz*. How do we know it?

10.   Which magazine was first published in September 1843 "to take part in a severe contest between intelligence, which presses forward, and an unworthy, timid ignorance obstructing our progress"?

11.   Mary Baker Eddy established this Church sponsored newspaper in 1908 as a protest against yellow journalism. Which one?

12.   What was striking about the crosswords appearing in the *Daily Telegraph* in Britain in 1944?

13.   "Television will never replace print. You can't swat a fly with a TV set, can you?" Who asked this very pertinent question?

Answers

1. Initially, soap manufacturers sponsored most of them on the radio.

2. The first crossword puzzle.

3. Practically all the people in Britain gathered around their television sets to watch the interview. But this was not directly responsible for the increased demand. After the telecast of the interview, most of them switched on their electric tea kettles so as to discuss things over a cuppa, and this caused the demand for power to shoot up!

4. Robert Maxwell.

5. *The Hindu*. Its front page used to carry only advertisements in those days.

6. Mashed potatoes! (Dan Quayle is requested to note the inclusion of the "e" in the spelling of the second word.)

7. *The Wall Street Journal*.

8. It is published every leap year on 29 February.

9. The television serial *Baywatch*.

10. *The Economist*.

11. *Christian Science Monitor*.

12. By a curious coincidence, the answers included many of the code-names used in the Normandy landings that were to take place later.

13. Alfred Hitchcock.

Mythological Matters

Myths are dramatic narratives about gods and men set in the remote past. They are a rich source of facts and details, and form the basis of the next few questions.

1.   They were the first race, the children of Uranus and Gaea. In different accounts their number varies, but a theory has gradually developed that there were twelve of them, as there were twelve great Olympian gods and goddesses. Most (some versions say all) brothers and sisters married each other. Who were they?

2.   When the three main Gods in Greek mythology divided the world, Zeus got the land, Hades the underworld and Poseidon the sea. In addition, Poseidon also got one part of the land in the world. Which region was this?

3.   The people of Phrygia, an ancient country of Asia Minor, were advised by the Gods to choose as king the first man they met on the way to Jupiter's temple. A peasant passed by, driving a wagon, and hailed as king to his great amazement, consecrated his wagon to Jupiter. Who was he?

4.   This Celtic deity, whose name meant "God of the People" was mentioned by the Roman poet Lucan in the first century. He had an unusual way of sacrificing his victims. He plunged them head first into a vat filled with a liquid, probably ale. Who was he?

5. She was so skilful in weaving that she challenged Athena to a weaving contest. When Athena ripped the cloth, she hanged herself in despair and was changed into a spider. Who was she?

6. He was a king of Cyprus and a celebrated sculptor. Thoroughly disgusted with the debauchery of females, he developed an aversion for women and resolved never to marry. He bestowed his affection upon a beautiful marble statue of a lovely girl, fell in love with it, and prayed to Aphrodite to give it life. She changed it into a woman, Galatea, whom he married. Whom are we referring to?

7. He was supposed to be the first king to reign over Italy. Having once offered his hospitality to Jupiter, he was endowed with the gift of knowing the past and the future. As the guardian of the gates, he is represented as having two faces, looking both ways. Who was this king, who has a month of the year named after him?

8. In Greek mythology, the son of Zeus was punished for revealing secrets by being placed in water up to his chin that receded when he tried to drink it, and under fruit-laden branches that drew back when he tried to pick the fruit. Which word is derived from his name?

Answers

1. The Titans.

2. Atlantis. The capital of this mythical land was called Poseidopolis in honor of Poseidon.

3.   Gordius, remembered for the "Gordian knot" by which he fixed his wagon to the temple.

4.   Toutatis, best known as the God called upon regularly by Asterix.

5.   Arachne. Spiders belong to the family of arachnids.

6.   Pygmalion, from whom George Bernard Shaw got the name of his famous play.

7.   Janus, after whom January is named.

8.   His name was Tantalus, and that is how we get the word "tantalize."

What's in a Name?

"A rose by any other name would smell as sweet," declaimed Shakespeare. Sure, but a bougainvillea by any other name would be easier to spell! The next set of questions is on names–both real ones and nicknames.

1. In Salman Rushdie's book *The Moor's Last Sigh*, the protagonist is named Raman Fielding. How did he get this surname?

2. Which word comes from the surname of a photographer in Federico Fellini's 1959 film *La Dolce Vita*?

3. Why did the Black rights activist Malcolm Little adopt the name Malcolm X?

4. Sunil Gavaskar was well known as the "Little Master." However, a certain other cricketer was also referred to by the same nickname. Who?

5. Charles Edouard Jeanneret adopted a pseudonym meaning "the crow-like one." What was it?

6. How did the state of Virginia get its name?

7. What name did Israel Beer Josephat take on his conversion from Judaism to Christianity?

8. By what name were the unruly and notorious soldiers belonging to the irregular battalions of the Turkish army referred to? Clue: Captain Haddock of Tintin comics.

9. What was the title given by King Edward I to his baby son in 1301?

10. What inspired Ian Fleming to coin the legendary code-name 007 for his secret agent, James Bond?

11. Who was so named because his mother was greatly influenced by Boris Pasternak's book *Doctor Zhivago*?

12. Which book was named after Anand Nagar, a lepers' colony in Calcutta?

13. In 1917, David Brewster named his invention by combining three Greek words that meant beautiful, form and watcher to get a name meaning "watcher of beautiful forms." What was it?

14. His name was Sir Percy Blakeney, but he was better known by another name–that of a small flower. Who was he?

Answers

1. His father was so eager to play cricket at the Bombay Gymkhana that he kept asking for "just one fielding."

2. Paparazzo, a term for a freelance photographer who aggressively and intrusively pursues famous people.

3. His guru, Elijah Mohammad, asked all Blacks to give up their "slave" surname and replace it with an X, to signify the African name of their forefathers which they could never know, as slaves used to take the surname of their masters.

4. Hanif Mohammed of Pakistan.

5. Le Corbusier.

6. It was named after Queen Elizabeth I, the Virgin Queen.

7. Paul Julius Reuter, of the news agency fame.

8.   Bashibazouks.

9.   Prince of Wales, a term by which the heir to the English throne has been known ever since.

10.   20007 is the zip code for the Georgetown area of Washington DC, where many CIA agents live.

11.   Boris Becker.

12.   *City of Joy* by Dominique Lapierre.

13.   It was the kaleidoscope, through which images could be observed. The Greek words from which it was derived were *kalos, eidos* and *skoptos.*

14.   The Scarlet Pimpernel.

Nobel Men and Women

The Nobel Prizes are presented annually on the anniversary of Alfred Nobel's death and have come to be regarded as the ultimate award a person can receive. Take this quiz and find out how much you know about the remarkable people who have won it.

1. Robert Lucas, the winner of the Nobel Prize for Economics in 1995 got to keep only half the one million dollars prize money. However, had he won the prize the next year, he would have kept the whole amount. Why was this? This has nothing to do with taxes!

2. He won the Nobel Prize for Physics in 1922 and dissolved the medal in acid to conceal it from the approaching Nazis in World War II. He developed the complementarity principle and was code-named Nicholas Baker in the Manhattan Project (the development of the atom bomb). Who was he?

3. Besides himself winning the Prize in Physics, eight of his students emulated this feat. Who was this man, who discovered a fundamental particle?

4. He advocated the use of large doses of Vitamin C to treat illness in man. He is the only man to win two Nobels outright, having won the 1952 Prize for Chemistry and the 1962 Peace Prize. The electronegativity scale bears his name and he is the author of the book *Nature of the Chemical Bond*, which is regarded as the Bible of Chemists. Who is this controversial scientist?

5.   She was born to Albanian parents in Skopje, Yugoslavia and baptized Agnes Gonxha Bojaxhin. She won the Nobel Peace Prize in 1979. By what name do we know her?

6,   Which Nobel Prize winning physicist started sketching in his later years and signed his sketches "Ofey" from "*Au fait*" meaning "It is done" in French?

7.   He gave all the money he got for winning the Nobel Prize to the Shrine of the Virgin in Cuba, where he lived, saying, "You don't have a thing until you give it away." Who was this generous man?

8.   Winner of two Nobel Prizes, she was the co-discoverer of an element and was the first person known to have died of radiation poisoning. Who was she?

9.   He never finished high school as he didn't care much for studies. He got a job as the community postmaster, but was dismissed because he spent most of his time reading and gossiping. In 1949, he won the Nobel Prize for Literature, and is perhaps remembered as much for his acceptance speech as for his work. Can you guess who he was?

10.   In 1859, this young Swiss banker visited Northern Italy, and was in the town of Castiglione when the French were fighting the Austrians at the Battle of Solferino. Appalled by what he saw, he campaigned for a universal recognition of the need to relieve suffering in war. As a result of his activities, the Geneva Convention was drafted in 1864. Name this person, who also set up a famous humanitarian organization and was awarded the 1901 Nobel Peace Prize.

11.   This mathematician and philosopher co-authored *Principia Mathematica*–a classic work on the logic of mathematics. He

made an appearance in the Hindi film *Aman* and was awarded the Nobel Prize for Literature in 1950. Who was he?

Answers

1. When Lucas divorced his wife in 1987, she got a clause added to the settlement stating that that she should receive half the Nobel Prize money if he won it before October 31, 1995. Lucas made it with a few weeks to spare!

2. Niels Bohr.

3. J. J. Thompson, discoverer of the electron.

4. Linus Pauling.

5. Mother Teresa.

6. Richard Feynman.

7. Ernest Hemmingway.

8. Marie Curie.

9. William Faulkner.

10. Henri Dunant, the founder of the Red Cross.

11. Bertrand Russell.

Musically Yours

Listening to music is a favorite pastime of many. If you're a music buff, then this section should be to your liking.

1.   Which British music group gets its name from the number of the government form that was to be filled by people seeking unemployment benefits?

2.   How do we better know the people with the surnames Yarrow, Storkey and Travers?

3.   Whenever Richard Wagner conducted the composer Felix Mendelssohn's music, he wore gloves. Why?

4.   The species *Australopithecus afarensis*, the earliest link in the human evolution chain, is said to date back 3.6 million years. What was the first fossil of this species popularly known as?

5.   David Bowie's song *Space Oddity* was released on June 11, 1969 to coincide with which event?

6.   The fastest selling record of all time is *John Fitzgerald Kennedy–A Memorial Album*, which sold four million copies in six days. When was it recorded?

7.   The Hawaiian word for "jumping flea" has given its name to a musical instrument that was originally Portuguese, but is now associated with the Hawaiian Isles. Which instrument is this?

8.   He was born Harry Rodger Webb in Lucknow in 1940 and was declared a Knight of the British Empire in July 1995–the first rock star to be so honored. Who is he?

9.   This band, formed in 1964, called themselves the *Warlocks*, not knowing there was another band with the same name. In search of a new appellation, one of the members opened a dictionary at random. The first thing he saw was a term for a traditional British folk ballad, in which a human helps the ghost of some-one who has died recently find peace. They gave themselves that name. Which band was this?

10.   The group *Europe* wrote and sung the song *Final Countdown* in memory of whom?

11.   A fire that swept through a casino in Montreux, Switzerland was the basis for which 1972 hit song by *Deep Purple*?

12.   He was brought up by his musical elder brother after their father died in 1695. He studied music passionately, creeping out of his bed to copy his brother's collection of music by the dim light of the moon. This ruined his weak eyesight and later led to his blindness. Who was this German composer?

13.   How did Eric Clapton's song *Layla* come about to be written? Clue: It had a great impact on the singer's personal life.

14.   In 1927, at the age of ten, Yehudi Menuhin played in Berlin with the Philharmonic Orchestra. After this famous performance, the boy found himself lifted up and kissed by a frail little man with a wild white mane. "Today, Yehudi, you have once again proved to me that there is a God in Heaven," the man said with tears streaming down his eyes. Who was this man?

Answers

1.   UB 40.

2.   Peter, Paul and Mary.

3.   Mendelssohn was a Jew and Wagner was an anti-Semite, so the latter thought it necessary to wear gloves.

4.   Lucy, from the *Beatles'* song *Lucy in the Sky with Diamonds*, which was popular with the exploration group that unearthed the fossil.

5.   The first lunar landing.

6.   November 22, 1963–the day Kennedy was assassinated.

7.   Ukulele.

8.   Cliff Richard.

9.   Grateful Dead.

10.   The crash victims of the space shuttle *Challenger*.

11.   *Smoke on the Water*.

12.   Johann Sebastian Bach.

13.   Eric Clapton and George Harrison were close friends. Unfortunately, Clapton fell in love with Harrison's wife, Pattie Boyd. The two friends decided to settle things through music. Both wrote a song each, but it was Clapton's song *Layla* that became a hit. Pattie Boyd became Mrs. Clapton.

14.   Albert Einstein.

Leading Edge

This section is on people who are or were Heads of State or Government. Little known facts about them are presented, so try and figure out who they are.

1.   As a 24 year-old journalist in South Africa, he was captured by the Boers in the Boer War. He escaped from the POW camp and a reward of 25 pounds was offered for his capture. Who was he?

2.   Which American President, conscious about his physical short-comings, wrote this limerick about himself:
>   For beauty I am not a star
>   There are others more handsome by far
>   But my face, I don't mind it
>   For I am behind it
>   It's the people in front that I jar!

3.   He is a civil engineer and has a boxer's nose from a boyhood brawl in which he caught a cart axle across the face. The thumb and forefinger on his left hand are missing, from the time in World War II, when he stole two hand grenades from an arsenal and tried to dismantle one with a hammer. Who is this man?

4.   As an 18 year-old during World War II, she joined the Auxiliary Territorial Service as an auto-mechanic. Officially she was no. Q30873. Who is she?

5.   The research for combating polio started in full swing only after a famous person was known to suffer from it. In fact, the polio vaccine might not have been discovered in 1955 had he not

helped found the National Foundation for Infantile Paralysis in 1937. Whom are we referring to?

6.   Who wrote a book for children titled *Al Karia al Karia: Al Ard al Ard (The Village the Village: The Land the Land)* to teach them the values of agricultural and rural life?

7.   As a youth in Poland in the 1930s, he was a budding actor and joined a theater troupe. He showed so much promise that his friends never doubted that he was going to become either an actor or a man of letters. During World War II, he worked as a laborer at a quarry operated by the German-run Solvay chemical firm on the outskirts of Krakow, where other workers called him "the student." Who is he?

8.   He was born in 1943 and educated at Rutlish Grammar School. He was an executive with Standard Chartered Bank from 1965 to 1969 and is an Associate of the Institute of Bankers. Can you guess who he is?

9.   At a banquet honoring 49 American Nobel laureates in 1962, President John F. Kennedy said: "This is the most extraordinary collection of human talent ever gathered at the White House, except perhaps when_____dined alone here." The person he was referring to, could calculate eclipses, survey an estate, draw blueprints for a building, break a horse, judge legal cases, dance a minuet, play the violin and launched the Republican Party. Who was he?

10. He was born in Branau, Austria, the son of a customs official. He dreamt of becoming a great artist, and upon the death of his beloved mother when he was 19, he set off for Vienna with in his own words, "a suitcase full of clothes in my hand and an indomitable will in my heart." The next four years were

abysmal ones. He was penniless, knew no trade and bounced from one job to another. When World War I started, he joined the German army and became a corporal. He was twice wounded and twice decorated, the second award being the Iron Cross, First Class, rarely given to enlisted men. Do you know who he was?

11. Which American President once patented a device for buoying ships to shoals, and even made a model of it, though a life-size version was never built?

12. Which French leader was the author of *Premier Accord*—a never published attempt at a romance novel, written in 1940?

Answers

1. Winston Churchill.

2. Woodrow Wilson.

3. Boris Yeltsin.

4. Queen Elizabeth II.

5. Franklin D. Roosevelt.

6. Col. Muammar Gaddafi.

7. Karol Wojtyla, now known as Pope John Paul II. Don't forget that the Pope is also the Head of the Vatican City State, and so his presence in this section is justified.

8. John Major.

9. Thomas Jefferson.

10. Adolf Hitler.

11.   Abraham Lincoln.

12.   Francois Mitterand.

In Capitals

This section is entirely devoted to capital cities of countries.

1. Apart from Washington DC, which capital is named after a US president?

2. Which African capital city's name literally means "new flower"?

3. Every state in this nation wanted its major city to be the capital. Finally, a new federal territory was created and the capital was developed by the American architect Walter Burley Griffin, whose plans won an international competition. Which capital city is this?

4. What is common to Aventine, Caelian, Capitoline, Esquiline, Palatine, Quirinal and Viminal?

5. Which city's name when translated from Spanish is "Holy Trinity and Harbor of Our Lady of Kind Winds"?

6. The site for this city was so carefully chosen that consideration was given to geology, climate, topography, soil, drainage, transportation, water supply, power, recreation, public administration, etc. Lucio Costa won the design competition for it, with plans for it in the form of a gigantic aircraft. Architect Oscar Niemeyer executed the plans to build one of the finest cities in the world. Which capital are we talking about?

7. The capital of which country is named after Lord Hanuman, the Hindu monkey God?

8.   Which is the only capital city in the world that is named after another capital city?

9.   How do we collectively know the three cities Leptis, Osa and Sabratha?

10.   The name of which Asian capital city means "muddy estuary"?

Answers

1.   Monrovia, the capital of Liberia, named after James Monroe.

2.   Addis Ababa, Ethiopia's capital.

3.   Canberra, the capital of Australia.

4.   They are the seven hills of Rome.

5.   (Santos Trinidad Puerto de Santa Maria de) Buenos Aires.

6.   Brasilia, the capital of Brazil.

7.   Brunei, whose capital is called Bandar Seri Begawan. "Bandar" is the Hindi word for "monkey."

8.   Tirana, the first city of Albania, named after Teheran (Iran).

9.   Tripoli, literally meaning "three cities."

10.   Kuala Lumpur.

The Written Word

The ascent of television has not dampened people's enthusiasm for books. For a bibliophile, there's nothing that compares with sitting down with an engrossing tome and being lost in its contents, oblivious of the passage of time. Are you such a person? Read on and find out.

1. We are little people, smaller than dwarfs. We love peace and quiet and good tilled earth. We dislike machines but are handy with tools. We are nimble and don't like to hurry. We have sharp eyes and ears, are inclined to be fat, wear bright colors and seldom wear shoes. We like to laugh, eat (six meals a day) and drink. If you still haven't identified us, we inhabit a land we call *The Shire*, a place between the River Brandywine and the Far Downs. Who are we?

2. In the original blurb for the first edition of this book in 1945, its author wrote: "It is the history of a revolution that went wrong–and of the excellent excuses that were forthcoming at every step for the perversion of the original doctrine." Which book is being referred to?

3. This mystery novel was written by 19 authors; each wrote a chapter building on the preceding one. The idea was conceived by publisher George Putnam. Which novel was this?

4. Which German book was written by a historical figure in a cell in Landsberg Prison?

5.   The idea for this famous work came to the author when he was lying drunk and penniless in an Austrian inn with a travel book by his side. Can you guess which work it is? Hint: Trilogy.

6.   What is peculiar about Erle Stanley Gardner's book *The Case of the Terrified Typist*?

7.   How do we better know Oliver Mellors?

8.   This book was rejected by 121 publishers before William Morrow & Co. accepted it in 1974. It thus holds the record for rejections before publication and consequent best-sellerdom. Name it.

9.   What is common to Dr. Joseph Bell, William Brodie, Delphene Delamare and Rev. Josiah Henson?

10.   It originated in a suggestion by the Dean Of Westminster in 1857 and was dedicated to Queen Victoria. It was completed in 1928 when copies were presented to King George of Britain and President Calvin Coolidge of the USA. Which work are we talking about?

11.   Which book was based on the true adventures of a Scottish soldier named Alexander Selkirk on the island of Juan Fernandez, off the coast of Chile?

12.   Which literary work was written at Prisengracht 263, Westerkirk, Amsterdam in 1942-43?

13.   What is the significance of the word "honorificabilitudinitatibus" which means "with honorableness" and occurs in Shakespeare's play *Love's Labor Lost*?

14. Ken Follet's book *On the Wings of Eagles* is an account of a certain person's 1979 mission to rescue two of his employees from an Iranian prison. Who was the individual?

15. Whose autobiography is aptly titled *The Final Condensation*?

Answers

1. The Hobbits, created by J. R. R. Tolkien.

2. *Animal Farm* by George Orwell.

3. Bobbed Hair

4. *Mein Kampf* by Hitler.

5. *The Hitchhiker's Guide to the Galaxy* by Douglas Adams. At latest count, the "trilogy" comprises five books.

6. This is the only case that Perry Mason loses in court.

7. As Lady Chatterley's lover.

8. *Zen and the Art of Motorcycle Maintenance* by Robert M. Pirsig.

9. All of them inspired great fictional characters–Sherlock Holmes, Dr. Jekyll & Mr. Hyde, Madame Bovary and Uncle Tom respectively.

10. *The Oxford English Dictionary*.

11. Daniel Defoe's *Robinson Crusoe*.

12. *The Diary of Anne Frank*.

13. It can be viewed as a rearrangement of the Latin sentence "Hi ludi F. Baconis nati tuiti orbi" meaning "These plays, F. Bacon's offspring, are preserved for the world." This is used to

support the theory that Francis Bacon actually wrote Shakespeare's plays.

14. Ross Perot.

15. De Witt Wallace, the founder of *Reader's Digest*, which carries condensed articles.

Holy Hollywood

In the 1800s, a property developer named Horace Wilcox bought a few acres of orange groves on the outskirts of Los Angeles. His wife named it Hollywood, after the home of a friend in Chicago. It is now the nerve center of the American film industry, and is the subject of the next few questions.

1.   Ian Fleming settled down in Jamaica and wrote most of his James Bond novels there. What was the name of his mansion there?

2.   *The Mousetrap* holds the record for being the longest running play in the world. When it was first staged, the lead character, Sergeant Trotter, was played by a person we all know as an eminent film personality. The female lead, Mollie Ralston, was played by a lady who went on to become his wife. Who was the man?

3.   Clark Gable was acclaimed for his performance as Rhett Butler in the film adaptation of Margaret Mitchell's book *Gone With the Wind*. The author's preference for the role, however, was someone else. Who?

4.   He directed his first film under the name Bob Roberts, since he was unsure of what the public's reaction would be. After the film proved to be a hit, his later films and re-releases of the first film were with his actual name. Which director are we talking about?

5.   She is the only performer to win four Oscars for starring roles, and was nominated twelve times. Her college career ended when

she was expelled from Bryn Mawr college for smoking a ciga-rette. Who is she?

6.   Whose screen-test result read: "Cute as a fox"?

7.   Only two Hollywood leading ladies never kissed their leading men on screen. One was the Chinese American star Anna May Wong. Who was the other?

8.   What was peculiar about the filming of Alfred Hitchcock's *The Rope*?

9.   What custom with regard to credit titles originated with the film *Death of a Gunfighter* in 1969, as a result of the high-handed behavior of the star, Richard Widmark, who had creative control?

10.   He was born to a Sicilian peasant family in 1897. To support his studies at the California Institute of Technology, he worked as an engine wiper, then recorded high praise for his contribution to an incendiary device that could burn more people than any previous device. He was a ballistics instructor during World War I, after which he did odd jobs and worked as a con-man. He bluffed his way into the film business and became one of Hollywood's leading directors. Who was he?

11.   He was born Israel Bailin in Tyumen, Russia in 1888, emigrated to America, and gave the catch phrase "No business like show business" to Hollywood. Can you figure out who he was?

12.   How would Western movie fans know George Parker and Harry Longbough better?

13.   Charlie Chaplin's film *Limelight*, made in 1952, won an Oscar for Best Original Score in 1972. Why did it take so long to win an Oscar?

14. Who made her big-screen debut starring as a real life cartoon character *Barb Wire* in the film of the same name?

15. During a promotion for the 1994 flop film *Stargate,* its director Roland Emmerich fielded a question about the existence of alien life. This gave him the idea to make another film. Which one was this?

Answers

1. Goldeneye.

2. Richard Attenborough.

3. Groucho Marx.

4. Sergio Leone. The film in question was *A Fistful of Dollars.*

5. Katharine Hepburn.

6. Michael J Fox.

7. Mae West.

8. It was filmed in one take.

9. Using the name Alan Smithee as a director's credit to cloak the identity of those who are so dissatisfied with the studio's handling of their work, that they refuse to be publicly associated with the film. Widmark's actions caused first Don Siegel and then his replacement Bob Totten to disclaim a personal credit. They persuaded the Director's Guild to allow a pseudonym. It was decided that using "Smith" would be making things too obvious, so "Smithee" was adopted instead!

10. Frank Capra.

11.   Irving Berlin.

12.   Butch Cassidy and the Sundance Kid.

13.   Only films released in the Los Angeles area during a year are eli-
       gible for the Oscar awards. *Limelight* was released in this region
       only in 1972.

14.   Pamela Anderson Lee, better known for her role in the televi-
       sion serial *Baywatch*.

15.   *Independence Day*. In fact, in one of the scenes in this movie, a
       bus is shown crashing through a billboard advertising *Stargate*.

War Clouds

Man has killed more fellow men than any other creature in history has. Never failing to unleash the forces of destruction to settle disputes, the many conflicts that have taken place also provide a fascinating trove of information.

1. In 1944, the BBC broadcast a line from a poem by Verlaine, which translated from French meant "wounds my heart with monotonous languor." What was the significance of this?

2. World War I was triggered off by the assassination of Archduke Francis Ferdinand of Austria by Gavrilo Princep. However, the Archduke might not have died and World War I might never have taken place had it not been for a peculiar habit the Archduke had. What?

3. During the Gulf War, the US soldiers were given packets of precooked food called MREs (Meals-Ready-to-Eat), which they found revolting. What jocular expression did they give to it?

4. During World War II, an inspector in Quiring, a Massachusetts ship-yard, chalked certain words on ships and equipment to keep people on their toes. These words eventually became the most ubiquitous of all graffiti. What were these words?

5. How do we better know Margaret Gertrude Zelle, a Dutch-Javanese dancer who was executed by a French firing squad during World War I?

6.   "This book is neither to be an accusation nor a confession and least of all an adventure, for death is not an adventure to those who stand face to face with it." Which book is this?

7.   The only British pilot to participate in the atomic bombings in World War II, he was so appalled by it that he set up a world-wide movement for the relief of suffering people. Who was he?

8.   He was a British soldier and archaeologist who fought in Arabia in World War I, after which he tried unsuccessfully to gain independence for the Arabs. He joined the Royal Air Force as an aircraftman under the name of Ross and later changed his name to Shaw. He was also a stylish writer who wrote of his war experiences in *The Seven Pillars of Wisdom*. Can you guess who he was?

9.   In 1859, a bloody battle was fought in Italy between a combined Franco-Sardinian army and an Austrian army. This battle gave its name to a red-purple dye and color synthesized shortly afterwards. Which color was it?

10.   Samuel Wilson, a local inspector of army supplies for the US Army during the War of 1812 has lent his name to which popular term?

11.   Who or what was Agent Orange?

12.   Which medal in the shape of the Maltese Cross, was originally made from metal of the cannons captured from the Russians at Sebastopol in the Crimean War?

Answers

1. It was a message to the French resistance that the Allied invasion of France would follow in the next 24 hours.

2. The Archduke was a very proud man and used to have his uniform stitched over him, so that there would not be a single crease to spoil his bearing. After he was shot, it was impossible to unbutton his uniform and by the time scissors were found, he had bled to death.

3. Meals Rejected by Ethiopians!

4. Kilroy Was Here.

5. Mata Hari, the great spy.

6. *All Quiet on the Western Front*–Erich Maria Remarque's classic novel set in the First World War.

7. Gp. Capt. Leonard Cheshire, who set up the Cheshire homes.

8. Lawrence of Arabia.

9. Magenta, the color of blood.

10. Uncle Sam.

11. It was a defoliating agent used by the US in the Vietnam War.

12. Victoria Cross.

Citius, Altius, Fortius

The Olympics were first held in 776 BC in Olympia to honor the Greek God Zeus. Emperor Theodosius ended the Games in 393 AD. Fifteen centuries later, they were revived due to the efforts of Baron Pierre de Coubertin, and the first modern Games were held in the capital city of Greece, Athens in 1896. "*Citius, Altius, Fortius*" meaning "Faster, Higher, Stronger" is the official motto of the Olympic Games.

1. Why were women not permitted to watch the ancient Olympics?

2. Who might have won the gold medal in the Pentathlon at the 1912 Olympic Games, if he hadn't performed dismally in shooting, in which he finished 21st out of the 32 participants?

3. His biological father was a Samoan. He was adopted by a Californian family, and being dyslexic, was branded retarded when young. Who is this Olympic gold medal winner, who revealed that he had AIDS?

4. The 1936 Berlin Olympics was marked by a massive propaganda effort by the Nazis. In a stage-managed dramatic gesture, which would later turn out to be very ironic as the Nazis went about conquering Europe, an olive branch was presented to Hitler by a very famous foreign athlete. Who was he?

5. Why did the rock band *Jack Mack and the Heart Attack* receive wide press publicity during the Atlanta Olympics in 1996?

6. In the 1986 Seoul Olympics, although Lawrence Clement of Canada finished 20th in yachting, he was awarded a silver medal. Why?

7.   Dorando Pietri won the marathon in the 1908 Games in London, but was disqualified for having been helped across the finish line by people including an eminent author. Who was this author?

8.   What is the rather unfortunate claim to fame of Moshe Weinberg in the Olympic scene?

9.   Why was the venue of the 1908 Olympics changed from Rome to London?

10. He was a member of Yale's Olympic gold medal winning rowing team in 1924 and ran for President of the United States in 1972. Whom are we referring to?

11. Why did Tommie Smith and John Carlos shoot into prominence after the 200 meters race of the 1968 Mexico Olympics?

12. What is common to James Connolly and Chattie Cooper with regard to the modern Olympics?

Answers

1.   Women weren't allowed to watch because the men competed in the nude!

2.   George Patton, the American General.

3.   Greg Louganis, the diver.

4.   Spyridon Louis, the Greek who won the first modern Olympic marathon at Athens in 1896.

5.   They were performing at Centennial Park when the bomb exploded there.

6.   He saved a fellow competitor from drowning.

7.   Arthur Conan Doyle.

8.   He was the first Israeli to be killed in the 1976 Munich Olympics massacre by Arab terrorists.

9.   The venue was changed due to the eruption of the volcano Vesuvius.

10.   Dr. Benjamin Spock, known for the child-care books he has written.

11.   They were the athletes who gave the black power salute at the victory podium.

12.   They were the first man and woman respectively to win an Olympic gold medal.

Terminological Exactitudes

The next quiz is on common phrases and terms, mostly concerning their origins.

1.   In days gone by, women were allowed to live in naval ships. If a woman gave birth to a child whose paternity was uncertain, what was the child entered in the log as?

2.   The Archbishop of Canterbury during the reign of Elizabeth I was a very inquisitive person. What term did this give rise to in the English language?

3.   What phrase did pilots of steamers on the Mississippi use to indicate that the water was up to the two fathom mark on their depth-finding line?

4.   In the olden days, when a jockey was winning a race by a large margin, he could afford to let go of the reins towards the end. What phrase thus arose?

5.   Which term for a group working for an enemy within a country at war came from General Mola's reference to such support in besieged Madrid in 1936?

6.   In the 9th century, the ruling Danes imposed a tax in Ireland. Those who neglected to pay it were punished by having their noses slit. What phrase did this give rise to?

7.   What term did a famous cartoon by Clifford K. Berryman, published in the *Washington Post* on November 16, 1902 contribute to the English language?

8.   The only certain way of discovering the age of a horse is by examining its lower jaw. What phrase derives from this?

9.   Which term meaning "enthusiastic" was a slogan adopted by the US Marines in 1942, from the Chinese word for "work together"?

10.   This phrase originates from Aesop's fable *The Milkmaid and her Pail*, about a woman who brings eggs to the market. She proclaims that she will buy a goose with the money she gets for her eggs, that with her profits from the goose she will buy a cow and so on. In her excitement, she kicks over her basket and the eggs break. Which phrase is this?

11.   The celebrated printer Aldus Manutius (1449-1515) employed a Black African as a helper in his shop in Venice. As Blacks were then unknown in that part of Europe, the people of Venice began to look upon him as an evil spirit. What term did this lead to?

12.   Which phrase was originated by Pope Gregory the Great for use during a particularly deadly 6th century epidemic?

13.   This term was introduced by Thomas Kuhn in his book *The Structure of Scientific Revolutions*, in which he showed that almost every significant breakthrough in the field of scientific endeavor was first a break with tradition and with old ways of thinking. Which term is this?

14.   A shepherd's staff has a bent piece of metal attached to one end, which is used to catch sheep by its leash. At the other end, it is bent in a "U" shape, which is used to catch sheep by the neck. What phrase has this given rise to?

15. In England in the past, a bowler who took three wickets on successive balls in a cricket game was entitled to something at the expense of the club. What?

Answers

1. Son of a gun, since women usually gave birth near the midship gun, behind a canvas screen.

2. Nosey Parker.

3. Mark Twain. Samuel Longhórne Clemens took his pen name from this.

4. Winning hands down.

5. Fifth column.

6. Pay through the nose.

7. Teddy bear, a parody on the then President, Theodore Roosevelt.

8. Straight from the horse's mouth.

9. Gung-ho, from "gonghe."

10. Don't count your chickens before they are hatched.

11. Printer's devil.

12. God bless you.

13. Paradigm shift.

14. By hook or by crook.

15. A hat, and hence the term "hat-trick."

Eureka

Discoveries are sometimes serendipitous, but most of the time they are the result of patient background work and a lot of plodding. As this quiz shows, they go a long way in improving our quality of life or increasing our understanding of the world around us.

1. Something all of us use regularly had its origin in a fierce rain-storm in 1564 that uprooted an immense tree in Borrowdale, England. What?

2. In 1861, a French naturalist named Henry Mouhot was pursuing an elusive butterfly in Indo-China, when he stumbled on what turned out to be one of the greatest discoveries of that century. What did he find?

3. Many Mayan cities of the past were discovered because the Indians worked hard to find a certain tree because of a particular habit in the United States. Which tree was this and what was the habit?

4. What was discovered on the first day of the 19th century–January 1, 1801–by G Piazzi, an Italian monk?

5. Legend has it that it was discovered by Kaldi, an Ethiopian goat-herd. What is it?

6. In January 1848, two men named John Sutter and James Marshall, while building a sawmill at the junction of the American and Sacramento rivers discovered something. What did this lead to?

7.   Doctors Luc Montagnier, J. C. Chermann and F. Barre Sinoussi discovered it at the Pasteur Institute in Paris in 1983. They called it the Lymphadenopathy Associated Virus because people afflicted with it were reported to have swollen lymph nodes. What are we referring to?

8.   One day in 1947, a fifteen-year-old Arab boy named Muhammad adh-Dhib went searching for a stray goat on a hillside near the northwestern corner of the Dead Sea. In a cove, he found several tall clay jars. What was inside them?

9.   What modern medium of communication was conceived by Paul Baran in 1964 at Rand Corporation as an answer to the problem of how orders could be issued in case of an all-out nuclear attack?

10.   The discovery of what was made in 2640 BC in the garden of Emperor Huang Ti?

11.   What important discovery was made by a nineteen year-old on a voyage to England from India aboard the ship *Lloyd Triestino* in August 1930?

12.   What idea did science fiction author Arthur C. Clarke propose in 1945 in the magazine *The Wireless World*?

13.   The world today spends billions on aerated soft drinks. Which scientist first dissolved carbon dioxide in water to make soda-water, a discovery for which he was awarded a gold medal?

14.   The idea for this was first conceived in London in September 1933 by the Hungarian theoretician Leo Szilard while he was walking in Bloomsbury. It was however achieved only in December 1942 in Chicago. What are we talking about?

Answers

1.   The pencil. In the cavity of the tree, they discovered a vast sup-
     ply of pure graphite, thought at the time to be a form of lead,
     and noticed that it could be used for writing.

2.   He found the remains of Angkor Wat.

3.   Sapodilla, from which chewing gum was made.

4.   Ceres, the first asteroid to be found. It is also the largest
     asteroid known.

5.   Coffee.

6.   Marshall had discovered gold, leading to the California Gold Rush.

7.   The AIDS virus.

8.   The Dead Sea Scrolls.

9.   The Internet.

10. Silk.

11. Chandrasekhar's Limit, the postulate that a star of mass greater
     than 1.4 times that of the sun (the Chandrasekhar limit) would
     end its life by collapsing into an object of enormous density
     such as a black hole.

12. The idea for the geostationary orbit for satellites 36,000 kilome-
     ters (22,400 miles) above the earth's surface.

13. Joseph Priestly, better known for his discovery of oxygen.

14. The world's first controlled self-sustaining nuclear chain reaction.

Searching for a Label

Have you ever wondered why something is called what it is? You'd be surprised to know that the reason, rather than always mundane, can sometimes be quite incredible, as this quiz will show you.

1. Combat 18 is an ultra-right group in Britain that targets Asians. Why do they call themselves Combat 18?

2. When Chinese scientists developed a herb-based drug to effectively combat heroin addiction, they named it 6.26. Why?

3. Why was the Winchester disk, a data storage device with high capacity, so called?

4. Tanks were first developed by the British during World War I and have since been used in battle-fields around the world. Do you know why they were named tanks?

5. Blue chip shares are regarded as a safe investment. They are those of the best performing and stable companies. Why are they labeled blue chips?

6. What was so named because a scientist remarked, "It's fat, and looks like Winston Churchill"?

7. At one point of time, Apple Computers was one of the world's most successful computer makers with their highly acclaimed Macintosh range. But, surely, Apple is a strange name for a company in the hi-tech computer business. How did it come to have a name like this? Clue: Spicy Indian food probably had something to do with it!

8.   The US Armed Forces' K-9 Corps was founded in 1942. Why was it designated K-9?

9.   Why was the Jerry can so named?

10.   When the bikini was first made, the marketing slogan called it the "smallest bathing suit in the world" and said it was not genuine unless it could be "pulled through a wedding ring." Why was it called the bikini?

11.   Why are sterile fruit flies called Tudor flies?

12.   When the sixteenth century Flemish geographer Gerardus Mercator published a book of maps detailing parts of Europe, he put on the cover a picture of a Greek titan holding the world on his shoulders. What was the name of this titan?

Answers

1.   The 1st and 8th letters in the English alphabet are A and H respectively, signifying the initials of Adolf Hitler.

2.   They named it after the United Nations designated date of June 26, when the world focuses on the problems of drug abuse.

3.   Because its original numerical designation corresponded to that of the Winchester rifle's caliber.

4.   While being built, the British called them "water tanks" to conceal their real purpose. The name remained even after their actual use was revealed in the Battle of the Somme against the Germans in 1916.

5.   Because the costliest chips in a casino are blue in color.

6.   Fat Man, the atomic bomb dropped over Nagasaki.

7.   Steve Jobs, after a visit to India, had severe dysentery and had to subsist on a diet of fruits (mostly apples) for a long time. So after he had founded a new firm with Steve Wozniak, what better way to pay tribute to the fruit that had been a part of his life for many months, than to name his company after it!

8.   The corps is composed of dogs (canines)!

9.   It was a kind of 5 gallon can first used by the Germans, who were referred to as "Jerry" by the Allies.

10.   It was named after the Bikini atoll, which was tiny but big news, because of the US hydrogen bomb testing there.

11.   They are called so after the English royal family of that name, which failed to produce any male heirs and died out with Queen Elizabeth I, who was childless.

12.   Atlas, which is why a collection of maps is called an atlas.

Pot-Pourri

Pot-pourri literally means "rotten pot" (which presumably contains a varied mixture of things). The following questions are eclectic in nature, all of them contributing to make a delectable hotch-potch.

1. Studying aerial photographs of Cuba in 1970, Henry Kissinger noticed something that convinced him the Russians were building a submarine base there. What was it that caught his attention?

2. What is keraunothnetophobia?

3. He was known as Trey when he was younger, though not any more. His official name is William Henry—the same as his father, grandfather and great-grandfather. He became a father in May 1996 and decided not to name the baby William if it had turned out to be a boy. Who is he?

4. What is the finest powder available in the world?

5. In the mid 1960s, Stanley Kubrick wanted from Lloyd's an insurance policy protecting against losses should something happen before the release of his film *2001: A Space Odyssey*. What did he want to insure against?

6. What is the significance of the number 4810 emblazoned on some Mont Blanc pens?

7. Who is the first man since Adam Smith to hold professorships in both Economics and Philosophy at Harvard?

8.   What is the accidental claim to fame of Oscar Pierce, a wealthy Texan farmer in the 1940s?

9.   Harry S Truman was the thirty-third President of the United States. What did the "S" in his name stand for?

10.   It was started in 1951 by Eric Morley, the Public Relations director of Mecca, a small leisure company which ran a series of dance halls in Britain, as a promotional campaign in an attempt to make his company the best leisure and catering group in Britain. What is it?

11.   In France, if a person wears a tiny red button on his lapel, what does it indicate?

12.   Fascinated with themes of betrayal, subterfuge and espionage, this English author is believed to have worked for British intelligence under Kim Philby during World War II. One of his best known stories, *Our Man in Havana*, is said to be based on his war-time experiences. Who was he?

13.   Which award was started in 1980 by a Swedish philatelist named Jakob von Uexkull, who sold his stamp collection to fund it?

14.   When an Elvis Presley stamp was issued in 1993, fans deliberately mailed letters with the stamp to non-existent addresses. Why did they do that?

15.   The leader of the first expedition to cross the entire continent of Antarctica by land, from sea to sea, is remembered for being the first man to do something else. Can you guess who he is?

Answers

1. He noticed new soccer fields and decided that it meant the Russians were at work–and play. Cubans play only baseball.

2. The fear of falling artificial satellites.

3. Bill Gates.

4. Solid helium. It consists of monatomic particles. Of course, it isn't just available to everybody!

5. The discovery of extra-terrestrial intelligence. Lloyd's didn't take the chance!

6. It is the height of Mont Blanc (in meters), the highest mountain in Europe.

7. Amartya Sen.

8. The Oscar statuette is named after him. His niece, Margaret Pierce, was a secretary at the Academy of Motion Picture Arts and Sciences. On seeing the unnamed statuette, she exclaimed, "Why, it looks just like my uncle Oscar!" The name stuck.

9. It did not stand for any single name, but for the names of both his grandfathers, which began with the letter "S."

10. The Miss World contest.

11. He has been awarded the *Legion d'Honneur*.

12. Graham Greene.

13. The Right Livelihood Award, also referred to as the Alternative Nobel Prize. Given a day before the Nobel awards ceremony, it

recognizes pursuits its founder believed were ignored by the Nobel Prizes.

14.   So that they would be sent back with the "Return To Sender" post-mark. *Return To Sender* was an Elvis song.

15.   Edmund Hillary, who wasn't quite content with conquering Mount Everest.

Parting Shots

"Dying is a very dull, dreary affair," commented Somerset Maugham. "My advice to you is to have nothing to do with it." Though people have by and large found it very difficult to heed Maugham's words, some have ensured that their last words live on after them.

1. Who is credited with the very appropriate last words: "Once I was waxing, and now I am waning"?

2. Which great economist, in the midst of a discussion, prophetically told his colleagues, "I believe we must adjourn this meeting to some other place"?

3. Whose last words were, "Goodbye, my friends, I go on to glory"?

4. This man was bold and arrogant to the last. "I'm ready to meet my Maker, whether my Maker is prepared for the ordeal of meeting me is another matter," he said. Who was this great world leader?

5. "I shall hear in heaven," mused this composer who had turned deaf in his later years. Who was he?

6. When this ex-Prime Minister was dying, he was asked whether he would like Queen Victoria to visit him. "No, it is better not. She would only ask me to take a message to Albert," he replied, referring to her late husband. Whom are we talking about?

7. "Kiss me Hardy," he said to his trusted lieutenant before passing away. His body was then preserved in a barrel of rum. Who was this great naval commander?

8. Facing defeat and humiliation as revolt and insurrection raged around him, he committed suicide, proclaiming, "What an artist the world is losing in me!" Who was this man who died as he had lived—with delusions of grandeur?

9. When the Roman army invaded Syracuse in 212 BC, they found this scientist and mathematician drawing figures in the sand. "Do not touch my circles," he commanded a soldier who asked him to get up. The soldier responded by killing him with a sword. Who was the scientist?

10. This author was bankrupt at the end of his life. When told how expensive an operation would be, he remarked, "Ah well, I suppose I shall have to die beyond my means." Name him.

11. This man had the last word on the subject. When his disciples asked him to say a few words for posterity's sake, he growled, "Get out! Last words are for those who haven't already said enough." Whom are we referring to?

Answers

1. The creator of the Waxworks Museum, Madame Tussaud.

2. Adam Smith.

3. Isadora Duncan, the American dancer and choreographer. She was about to test-drive a Bugatti car, and was strangled when the scarf she was wearing got caught in the spokes of a wheel.

4. Winston Churchill.

5. Beethoven.

6. Benjamin Disraeli.

7.   Horatio Nelson.

8.   Emperor Nero.

9.   Archimedes.

10.   Oscar Wilde.

11.   Karl Marx.

The A to Z of Quizzing

The end of this book is near, and to purloin Virginia Slims' catch phrase, I hope "You've come a long way, baby!" This last section has 26 questions, the answers to which begin with the letters of the English alphabet from A through to Z. So keep track of the letters and work your way through it. Good luck!

1. Which is the oldest existing Parliament in the world?

2. It was first made out of two handkerchiefs and some ribbon by a New York debutante named Mary Phelps Jacob and her French maid. What was it?

3. In Greek myth, it was the rude and shapeless mass whose appearance could not be described, for there was no light by which it could be seen. It existed before the formation of the Universe and from it a Supreme Power created the world. What was it called?

4. Which rock group takes its name from the villain of the film *Barbarella*?

5. Who designed the Statue of Liberty?

6. This word is derived from the Italian word for a bottle. It was used by the glassblowers of Venice to describe bad workmanship, and it may have an allusion to the bursting of a bottle. Which word is it?

7. Who was the first man to cross the Mediterranean Sea by air in 1913?

8.   The members of this tribe in Kashmir have baffled scientists because they are seemingly immune to cancer. Which tribe is this?

9.   In ancient Greece, a private citizen who was not engaged in any public office was regarded as an uneducated and ignorant individual. What was he called?

10. Which psychologist coined the term "synchronicity"?

11. In skittles, the pin at the front apex, if struck successfully knocks down all the others. What is it called?

12. A serious artist and expert water colorist, he gave drawing lessons to Queen Victoria. His topographical designs were so accurate that experts recognized the geology of a country from his sketches. He is unquestionably the father of the limerick. Who was he?

13. At the age of five, he composed the music for *Twinkle Twinkle Little Star*. Who was this child prodigy?

14. Which popular brand of footwear is named after the Greek Goddess of Victory?

15. Which organization started in a room above a laundry on Banbury Road in Oxford in 1942, to plan a campaign to end famine in Greece?

16. Who was the blind Benedictine monk who gave his name to the first truly sparkling champagne?

17. What is the fruit from which marmalade was originally made, and from which it gets its name because the Portuguese name of the fruit was "marmale"?

18. If you're a fan of the *Superbowl*, you have him to thank. He also co-invented *Monday Night Football*, the second longest running prime-time show on American TV. Who is he?

19. It was announced on March 13, 1953 that 672,058,000 copies of the works of Marshal Josef Vissarionovich Dzhugashvili had been sold and distributed in 101 languages. How is he known to us?

20. Who has created a successful line of perfume called *Passion*?

21. According to Chinese legend, it was invented by the wife of a Chinese carpenter named Lou-Pan. It was introduced into England for personal use by Jonas Hanway. What are we talking about?

22. In German myth, which creatures are supposed to hover around the heads of warriors who die in battle?

23. If Clint Eastwood was good and Lee Van Cleef was bad, then who was ugly?

24. The man who won the first Nobel Prize for physics in 1901 for a discovery that revolutionized science, refused to make any money out of it and died a pauper. What did he discover?

25. In a strange land in the South Seas, Gulliver sees disgusting half-human, half-ape creatures controlled by horses called Houyhnhnms (the spelling is right!). Who were these creatures?

26. What is the branch of applied chemistry dealing with the use of fermentation in brewing, etc? Clue: It is the last word in many dictionaries.

Answers

1.   Althing (Iceland).

2.   Bra.

3.   Chaos.

4.   Duran Duran.

5.   Eiffel, Gustave.

6.   Fiasco.

7.   Garros, Roland.

8.   Hunza.

9.   Idiot.

10.   Jung, Carl.

11.   King-pin.

12.   Lear, Edward.

13.   Mozart, Wolfgang Amadeus.

14.   Nike.

15.   Oxfam.

16.   Perignon, Dom.

17.   Quince.

18.   Rozzelle, Pete.

19.   Stalin.

20.   Taylor, Elizabeth.

21. Umbrella.

22. Valkyries.

23. Wallach, Eli.

24. X rays.

25. Yahoos.

26. Zymurgy.

Afterword

It is possible that some inaccuracies may have crept into this book. Please rest assured if you find anything you feel does not conform to facts. It is not a deliberate attempt to malign anyone or mislead you. I would be grateful if you would bring any such items to my notice.

Did you enjoy this book? Is there any way in which it can be improved? I'd be glad to hear from you.

Write to me at:
Ranjit Thomas
C/o iUniverse.com
37 West 19th Street
6th Floor
New York, NY
10011-4200

Or simply email me at quizzing@hotmail.com.